BEAUTIFUL BEADWORK
from
NATURE

BEAUTIFUL BEADWORK

from

NATURE

16 Stunning Jewelry Projects Inspired
by the Natural World

Melissa Shippee

LARK
New York

An Imprint of Sterling Publishing Co., Inc.
1166 Avenue of the Americas
New York, NY 10036

LARK CRAFTS and the distinctive Lark logo are registered trademarks
of Sterling Publishing Co., Inc.

ISBN 978-1-4547-1077-6

Distributed in Canada by Sterling Publishing Co., Inc.
c/o Canadian Manda Group, 664 Annette Street
Toronto, Ontario M6S 2C8, Canada
Distributed in the United Kingdom by GMC Distribution Services
Castle Place, 166 High Street, Lewes, East Sussex BN7 1XU, England
Distributed in Australia by NewSouth Books
University of New South Wales, Sydney, NSW 2052, Australia

For information about custom editions, special sales, and premium and
corporate purchases, please contact Sterling Special Sales at 800-805-5489
or specialsales@sterlingpublishing.com.

Manufactured in Canada

2 4 6 8 10 9 7 5 3

sterlingpublishing.com
larkcrafts.com

Interior design by Shannon Nicole Plunkett
Cover design by David Ter-Avanesyan
Photography by Chris Bain

GettyImages/iStock: Amphora: 141; Kick images: 49; LesyaDL: 27; LianeM: 39;
SW_Olson: 87; Alan Phillips: 99; Pixel Digits: 115; User2547783c_812: 71;
Wacharaphong/iStock: 33; **Pixabay:** dimitrisvetsikas1969: 63; dschmunis: 21; Hans: 109;
Kasabubu: 149; kellyclampitt: 17; Pexels: 79; **Vibly Photo/Shutterstock:** 125

Contents

Introduction

The natural world is not only infinitely fascinating to study but also a wonderful source of interesting color combinations, shapes, textures, and patterns. As long as I can remember, I've always been amazed by how the observable world works and have found beauty in its visual aspects. I was blessed to have grown up in a rural area, where I could find patches of undeveloped and intrinsically wild land that has been untouched by human endeavor. All I've had to do to come face-to-face with unending sources of inspiration is to step out of my back door.

My relationship with nature is not unique; there is a deep and inherent need in all of us to connect with the natural world, the world that is somehow apart or other from human influence. For millennia, humans have used handicrafts as a way to capture imagery from nature. From the earliest prehistoric cave paintings and the ancient metalwork created by ancient Egyptians, to the elaborate hand- and machine-sewn clothing of the Victorian era and the artwork of Impressionist painters, you can find bits of inspiration pulled from the natural world in every artistic endeavor and craft imaginable.

Beading (and, more specifically, beadweaving) is an ideal medium for creating pieces of art that incorporate themes, shapes, colors, and patterns drawn from nature. The materials that are used for bead weaving are incredibly beautiful and intrinsically pleasurable to work with, but they become elevated when used in a way that evokes imagery from the natural world. The beading projects within these pages are inspired by animals, plants, flowers, microscopic imagery, geology, astronomical phenomena, and other observable wonders of the natural world. And I've included all the resources and instructions needed to bring these pieces to life.

The Tools & Materials and Techniques sections explain what you'll need to complete each one. The subsequent parts of the book contain projects for different kinds of jewelry: necklaces, bracelets, and smaller accessories, such as earrings or a brooch. Beaders with experience creating intermediate-level projects will find new and challenging techniques in each project, while beaders with less experience will find projects that are easier to master at the beginning of each section and can then build their skills with the more difficult projects toward the end of the section. I hope beaders at any skill level will find inspiration in the design, color patterns, and the intricate detail found in the pieces throughout the book.

No matter which projects you choose, the jewelry you create will become pieces that you have made with well-chosen materials and engaging techniques. They'll be stunning works of nature-inspired art to be proud of, to be cherished, and to be appreciated throughout the generations.

Tools
&
Materials

Tools

BEADING SURFACE

Arguably the most important tool that you will use is a beading surface. Your surface should allow you to spread out your beads so you can easily pick them up with your needle. There is a large variety to choose from, ranging from simple and inexpensive versions to ones that are artfully decorated and pricier.

The simplest and most common beading surface is often referred to as a beading mat, which consists of a rectangular piece of Vellux®, a reversible fabric that has a soft, fuzzy appearance. Vellux has a core of thin polyester foam; nylon hairs are attached to the foam on both sides at a 90-degree angle. These hairs are long and stiff enough to allow you to easily maneuver a needle through the holes of your bead without catching it on the polyester core, making this an ideal surface for beading. Vellux beading surfaces are often sold at local bead shops and are very inexpensive.

There are many other beading surfaces produced in a factory setting or made lovingly by hand. They range from storage cases with built-in beading surfaces that hold a project in place for travel to cushioned, decorated, and ergonomic surfaces designed to sit on a lap. Some take the form of sticky gel-like sheets designed to hold your beads in place. The sizes of these products span from just a few inches in width and length to more than a foot (30.5 cm) across.

No one beading surface is superior to the others; they all have their benefits and shortcomings. The beading surface you choose should be the one on which you feel the most comfortable working, no matter what situation you may find yourself beading.

NEEDLES

It's a good idea to keep your beading kit stocked with a variety of beading needles. Beading needles are usually of Japanese or English origin. Unlike ordinary sewing needles, they have an eye whose diameter does not exceed the width of the needle's shaft. This allows them to pass easily through beads, even if you're needle is holding two strands of thread.

Beading needles are sized like wire gauges; the smaller number sizes denote thicker needles and the larger number sizes denote thinner needles. Sizes 10, 11, 12, and 13 are most commonly used for beading projects that include many size 11° and 15° Japanese seed beads. Smaller needle sizes, such as the hair thin size 15 beading needle, may be needed in select projects that utilize size 14° or 15° Czech seed beads, which are even smaller than size 15° Japanese seed beads. Size 12 beading needles are my go-to needle size for 90 percent of the projects I complete. They are sturdy and do a great job of passing through size 15° and 11° seed beads without wearing out quickly.

No matter what size needle you are using, you will need to have extras on hand. Over time, beading needles will bend and eventually break from all the strain caused by pulling your thread tightly or taking up the slack in your beadwork.

SCISSORS

You can use any type of scissors to cut beading thread, as long as they are sharp enough to do the job. I like to use small, inexpensive sewing scissors that fit inside a box that I can carry around and keep with the rest of my beading tools. Keep in mind that fishing line thread will eventually dull the blade on most types of scissors. Some companies manufacture specialty cutters or scissors designed for fishing line thread, but I have found that my sharp, small scissors do the job well enough. When they stop working as well as I would like, I just buy a new pair!

BEAD SCOOPER

Inevitably, you will need to clean up a spill of beads or put beads back into a small tube or bag when you've finished using them. In those instances, a bead scooper is absolutely indispensable. It makes these tasks much quicker to complete and is more efficient than using your hands. I prefer the small metal triangular version of this tool as it is easy to handle and funnels beads into small openings.

PLIERS

Pliers are not completely necessary for most beadweaving projects, but they are useful for pulling needles through tightly filled bead holes, breaking beads that were added accidentally, and straightening bent beading needles. In addition, they can be used to set crystal stones into settings, which can eliminate the need to create beaded bezels for large stones. Flat-nose or chain-nose pliers, which have a flat surface on the inside of their jaws, are the best choice for these uses.

BEADING AWL

Like pliers, the beading awl is not an essential tool, but it is incredibly useful for two tasks: removing beads from your beadwork and undoing beading stitches. An awl allows you to break a bead from the inside out, which prevents sharp pieces of the bead from cutting the thread. Its pointed tip is also ideal for picking thread out from between beads.

TAPE MEASURE

Tape measures, particularly the flexible plastic kind that retract into a circular storage unit, are helpful for measuring the dimensions of finished projects and the materials that you're using.

Beader's Tool Kit

I keep a small portable box with everything that I need to work in it. It comes with me wherever I'm working on a project. These are the items inside:

- Needles
- Scissors
- Bead triangle or scooper
- Pliers
- Beading awl
- Small spools of thread
- Tape measure

Materials

THREAD

There are many different brands and types of beading thread on the market, but they all fall into two basic categories: nylon thread and fishing line thread. Nylon thread is great for projects where flexibility is desired. Fishing line thread is better for projects that need more tensile strength or that will experience more strain while being worn, such as very heavy pieces. Among the different types of fishing line threads, I prefer to use the braided variety because of its superior strength and resistance to fraying.

SEED BEADS

Beadweaving is all about seed beads! These tiny glass beads form the structural basis for most beadwoven projects. Most seed beads on the market are manufactured in Japan, Czech Republic, and China. I prefer Japanese seed beads because their sizing is consistent, and there is an incredible array of sizes, finishes, and colors available. Since the sizing of Japanese beads is slightly different from those produced in the Czech Republic, it's best to stick with Japanese seed beads.

CYLINDER BEADS

Though technically a type of seed bead, cylinder beads have a distinctly different shape. Their walls are the same width from top to bottom, creating a symmetrical tube. These beads are wonderful for creating structure in beadweaving because they fit together like bricks.

PRESSED GLASS BEADS

You can find all different sizes, shapes, colors, and finishes of glass beads produced in many places around the world. I am partial to Czech glass beads as they are made using the same techniques that have been used for centuries to create very high-quality beads with a stunning array of colors and finishes. The most common sizes range from about 3 mm to 10 mm or larger.

TWO-HOLE BEADS

Though they are technically a type of pressed glass beads, two-hole beads deserve their own category. The second hole allows you to add them to beadwork in a way that wouldn't be possible with just one hole. You can find many types of two-hole beads, including Duo beads, tile beads, two-hole daggers, and two-hole cabochons.

CRYSTAL STONES

Crystal stones are one of my favorite materials to use as a focal point in my designs. The highest quality crystal stones are made in Austria and mimic the look of gemstones, but they come in a much wider range of shapes, colors, and finishes. They add a touch of glamour to projects that primarily use seed beads, for a fraction of the cost of a natural stone, and they look just as good or even better.

CRYSTAL BEADS

Like crystal stones, crystal beads come in a wide variety of shapes, sizes, and colors. The highest quality ones are also made in Austria. Since they have holes, they add a touch of sparkle to beadweaving projects without the need to create structure to hold them in place. My favorite crystal beads to use are bicones and faceted rounds.

CRYSTAL PEARLS

Crystal pearls are an amazing replacement for freshwater pearls, which are getting more difficult to find in different colors because of environmental and economic concerns. These beads can dress up an ordinary seed bead project and turn it into something very special. I always keep a large variety of 3-mm and 4-mm round pearls on hand as these are the most common shape and sizes to use in beadweaving projects.

FINDINGS

Findings are the metal jewelry components, such as ear wires, head pins, clasps, jump rings, and pin backs, that can be used to finish bead-woven projects. You'll find the quality of these items can vary greatly depending on the manufacturer and materials, but more often than not, local bead stores will carry the higher-end options.

Techniques

Project Difficulty Levels

LOW INTERMEDIATE

The projects at this difficulty are well suited for those who have tried multiple beadweaving stitches and are comfortable with the basic techniques for starting and ending threads.

INTERMEDIATE

This difficulty level is for those who are comfortable with most beadweaving stitches, have completed several projects in the past, and are ready for a new challenge or technique.

ADVANCED INTERMEDIATE

This difficulty level is for those who have used most of the beadweaving stitches in a variety of combinations and have finished many projects on their own.

ADVANCED

Advanced projects are for those who have been beading for several years; completed many projects involving different stitches, variations of stitches, and combinations of stitches; and possibly even designed some projects of their own. These projects offer unique combinations of techniques that will further the advanced beader's skill set even more.

Measuring Thread

When you begin a project, you'll often be asked to "needle up a wingspan of thread." To do so, hold the spool of thread in one hand and grasp the thread in the other, then stretch your arms apart so that they are the furthest apart they can be, like a bird in flight. This length is approximately equal to your height.

Peyote Stitch

Peyote stitch is often the first stitch a beader learns. It's versatile and provides a strong structural base for embellishment. It can also be easily combined with other beading stitches. The first strung "row" forms the first two counted rows of your beadwork (i.e., rows 1 and 2). There are two ways to count the rows. You can count the beads that ascend like steps from left to right or right to left. Alternatively, count the beads on the leftmost and rightmost edges, then add those two tallies together for even-count peyote. Do the same and subtract one for odd-count peyote. Flat peyote stitch requires reversing the stitching direction, or doing a "turnaround" at the end of each row. Tubular peyote stitch does not require turnarounds, but you will need to "step up" at the end of each row to position the thread for the next round.

EVEN-COUNT FLAT PEYOTE STITCH

1. Needle up your thread of choice. Pick up one bead; this will serve as a stop bead that holds the other beads in place as you work. Bring the stop bead down to the end of the thread, leaving a tail of at least 4 inches (10.2 cm). Stitch through the bead again to anchor it. Pick up an even number of the pattern beads and bring them down against the stop bead **(Fig. 1)**. Half of these strung beads will form the first row of the peyote stitch, and the other half will form the second row.

2. To start the third row, pick up a bead. Skip over the last bead added previously and stitch through the one after it, working in the direction toward the stop bead **(Fig. 2)**.

3. Pick up one bead, skip the next bead, and stitch through the one after it. Repeat until you've reached the end of the row and stitched through the first bead strung **(Fig. 3)**.

4. For the next row, you'll start with the basic even-count turnaround. Pick up a bead, skip the bead from which your thread is emerging and stitch through the next bead added in the previous row. Repeat the process until you reach the end of the row **(Fig. 4)**.

5. Continue stitching rows by repeating steps 3 and 4 for the length indicated by the pattern. You can remove the stop bead whenever you feel comfortable or when the beads seem like they won't come loose at the beginning of the stitch.

ODD-COUNT FLAT PEYOTE STITCH

1. Needle up your thread of choice. Pick up one bead to use as a stop bead or hold onto your tail thread. (The figures show the peyote stitch with a stop bead.) Bring the stop bead down to the end of the thread, leaving a tail of at least 4 inches (10.2 cm). Stitch through the bead in the same way again to anchor it. Pick up an odd number of the pattern beads and bring them down against the stop bead. As with the even-count peyote stitch, half of these strung beads will form the first row, and the other half will form the second row.

2. To start the third row, pick up a bead, skip the last bead added previously, and stitch through the one after it in the direction toward

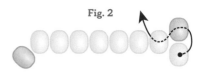

Fig. 1

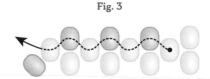

Fig. 2

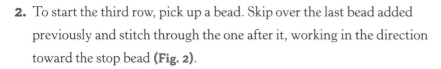

Fig. 3

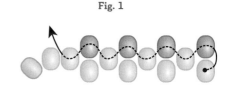

Fig. 4

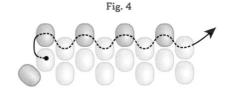

Fig. 1

Fig. 2

the stop bead. Repeat to add additional beads until your thread emerges from the second to last strung bead in the previous row **(Fig. 1)**.

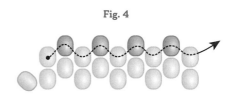

Fig. 3

3. Pick up a bead and stitch into the first strung bead in the direction away from the stop bead **(Fig. 2, blue thread)**.

4. The fourth row will have an even number of beads. To set up your thread in the correct location and direction to add the next row, you will need to complete an odd-count turnaround. Stitch through the next two beads **(Fig. 2, pink thread)** and the bead above or below the one through which you just passed **(Fig. 2, purple thread)**. Stitch through the next two beads in the previous rows, working in the direction toward the stop bead **(Fig. 2, black thread)**. Reverse direction and stitch through the last bead that you added **(Fig. 3)**.

Fig. 4

5. Pick up a bead, skip the bead after the one where your thread is emerging, and stitch through the one after that in the direction away from the stop bead. Continue stitching in this way until you reach the end of the row. Your thread will emerge from the end bead in the previous row **(Fig. 4)**.

6. Repeat steps 2 and 3 to stitch the fifth row and do an odd-count turn.

7. Repeat steps 5 and 6 to continue stitching as many odd and even rows as the pattern dictates. You can remove the stop bead whenever you feel comfortable and when it seems as though the first few beads in the pattern are secure and will not come loose.

TUBULAR PEYOTE STITCH

1. Needle up your thread of choice and pick up an even number of beads. Stitch through the first two or three beads to form a loop **(Fig. 1)**.

Fig. 1

2. Pick up a new bead, skip the next bead in the loop, and stitch through the one after that. Repeat from the beginning of this step until you've stitched through the last bead in the loop **(Fig. 2)**.

3. To step up, which moves your thread in position for the next round, stitch through the first bead which you added in step 2 **(Fig. 3)**.

Fig. 2

Fig. 3

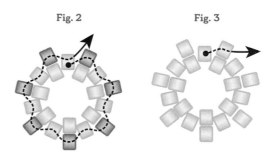

4. Continue adding rounds of beads using tubular peyote stitch and stepping up at the end of each row as your pattern dictates.

Netting

Netting can come in many different forms, depending on how many beads are needed in each stitch. There is no one way to make it. This is just one example that will be helpful for the projects in this book.

Fig. 1

1. Needle up your thread of choice and pick up the number of beads specified by your pattern.

2. Pick up three beads, skip over the last three beads added, and stitch through the fourth bead back. *Pick up three beads, skip over the next three beads in the initial row, and stitch through the fourth bead. Repeat from the * until you stitch through the last bead in the initial row (**Fig. 1**).

Fig. 2

3. To start a new row, pick up five beads and stitch through the middle bead in the last group of three added. *Pick up three beads and stitch through the middle bead in the next group of three beads in the previous row. Repeat from the * to complete the rest of the row (**Fig. 2**).

4. Repeat step 3 until your netting is the desired length.

Ladder Stitch

Ladder stitch, or laddering, can be used to build beadwork or to attach two pieces of beadwork together.

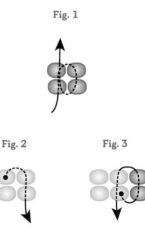

Fig. 1

1. To build beadwork, you can start with any number of beads. The following steps and illustrations show two beads per row. Pick up two pairs of beads (four beads in total). Stitch through the first pair of beads a second time in a circular fashion, holding onto your tail thread or using a stop bead so the beads don't fall off the tail. This establishes the first two rows of ladder stitch (**Fig. 1**).

Fig. 2   Fig. 3

2. Stitch through the second pair of beads again to prepare to make the next row (**Fig. 2**).

3. Pick up two beads and stitch through the previous pair of beads in a circular fashion (**Fig. 3**).

Fig. 4

4. Stitch through the last pair of beads again to prepare to make the next row (**Fig. 4**).

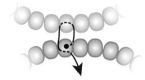

Fig. 5

5. Continue adding pairs of beads following steps 3 and 4 until you have the desired number of rows. You can build additional beadwork, like a herringbone tube, off of these laddered rows.

6. To use ladder stitch to connect two pieces of beadwork together, you'll use the same type of circular thread path without adding any new beads. Bring your thread out of the bead or beads you wish to attach to a second piece of beadwork. Stitch through the bead in the second piece of beadwork, then through the bead in the first piece of beadwork in a circular fashion. It's ideal to repeat the thread path at least once to reinforce the connection, or to connect other sets of beads as well so there are more threads to hold the connection together **(Fig. 5)**.

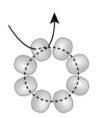

Fig. 1

Tubular Herringbone Stitch

Although there are many types of herringbone stitch, tubular herringbone stitch is the only one that will be used in this book.

1. Needle up your choice of thread and pick up eight beads. Stitch through the first bead again to form a ring **(Fig. 1)**.

Fig. 2

2. Pick up two beads and stitch through the next bead in the loop. Skip the next two beads and stitch through the third **(Fig. 2, blue thread)**. Pick up two beads and stitch through the next bead. Skip the next two beads in the loop and stitch through the third **(Fig. 2, red thread)**. Stitch through the first bead in the first pair added to step up **(Fig. 2, green thread)**. Pull the working thread and the tail thread in opposite directions to form two herringbone ladders.

3. To add a row to the ladder, pick up two beads and stitch down through the next bead in the first ladder. Then stitch through the first bead in the second ladder **(Fig. 3a)**. Pick up two beads and stitch down through the next bead in the second ladder **(Fig. 3b)**.

Fig. 3a   Fig. 3b

4. To step up, stitch through the top two beads in the first ladder **(Fig. 4)**.

5. To continue building rows, repeat steps 3 and 4 until the herringbone tube is the desired length.

Fig. 4

Right-Angle Weave (RAW)

Right-angle weave can have different numbers of beads in each unit. The instructions here show you how to make a unit with four beads, which is the most basic form.

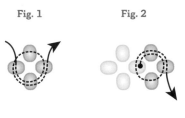

Fig. 1   Fig. 2

1. Needle up your thread of choice and pick up four beads. Stitch through the first bead again to form a loop, leaving a tail at least 4 inches (10.2 cm) long. Then stitch through the next two beads so your working thread is opposite your tail thread **(Fig. 1)**. This is your first unit.

2. Pick up three beads and stitch through the bead from which your thread is emerging again to form a loop, then stitch through two more beads **(Fig. 2)**. This is your second unit.

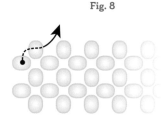

Fig. 3

3. Repeat step 2 until your first row has the number of units needed.

4. To step up, stitch through the top bead of the last unit **(Fig. 3)**.

5. Pick up three beads. Stitch through the top bead in the last unit, then the first new bead added **(Fig. 4)**.

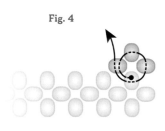

Fig. 4

6. Pick up two beads. Stitch through the top bead in the second to last unit of the first row, working toward the first added unit in the second row **(Fig. 5)**. Stitch through the next bead in the previous unit, then the two new beads added. Stitch through the bead on the edge of the next unit in row 1 **(Fig. 6)**.

7. Pick up two beads and stitch through the side bead in the previous unit in the row, then the top bead of the next unit in row 1. Then stitch through the first new bead added **(Fig. 7)**.

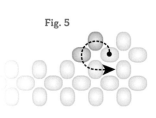

Fig. 5

8. Repeat steps 6–8 until you reach the end of the row. To complete the row and step up, stitch through the top bead in the last unit added **(Fig. 8)**.

9. To add additional rows, repeat steps 5–9.

Fig. 6   Fig. 7   Fig. 8

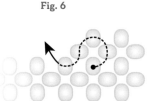
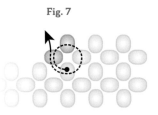

Cubic Right-Angle Weave (CRAW)

Like flat right-angle weave, cubic right-angle weave can have any number of beads in each side of each unit. The most basic form has four beads in each side, which is what is shown here. Cubic right-angle weave is also known as the four-sided prismatic right-angle weave.

1. Needle up your thread of choice and pick up four beads. Stitch through the first bead again to form a loop, leaving tail at least 4 inches (10.2 cm) long. Stitch through the next three beads and the first bead again. Retrace the thread path one more time to hold the beads firmly in place **(Fig. 1)**. This is the base of the first unit, or what some call the "floor" of the four-sided cubic unit.

2. Pick up three beads and stitch through the bead in the base from which the thread is emerging again. This is the first side of the unit. Continue stitching into the next bead in the base **(Fig. 2)**.

3. Pick up two beads and stitch down through the nearest bead on the first side. Stitch through the bead in the base from which your thread is emerging, then the next bead in the base **(Fig. 3)**. This is the second side.

4. For the third side, pick up two beads and stitch down through the nearest bead on the second side. Stitch through the bead in the base from which your thread is emerging **(Fig. 4)**.

5. Stitch through the next bead in the base, then up through the next bead in the first side, working away from the base **(Fig. 5)**.

6. To add the final side, pick up one bead and stitch down through the nearest bead in the third side. Stitch through the next bead in the base, then up through the next bead in the first side **(Fig. 6)**.

7. To step up, stitch through the top bead of the first side **(Fig. 7)**.

8. Stitch through the four beads on the top of the unit to bring them together. This completes your first CRAW unit. These four beads form the base of the next unit **(Fig. 8)**.

9. Repeat steps 2–8 to build as many additional units as needed.

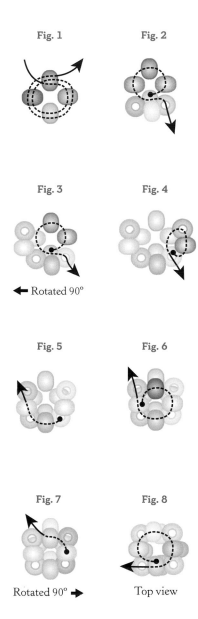

Fig. 1   Fig. 2

Fig. 3   Fig. 4

← Rotated 90°

Fig. 5   Fig. 6

Fig. 7   Fig. 8

Rotated 90° →   Top view

Prismatic Right-Angle Weave (PRAW)

This stitch is made the same way as cubic right-angle weave, but with a different number of sides. While the stitch can have any number of beads in each side of each unit, the most basic form, which has four beads in each side of each unit, is shown here.

THREE-SIDED PRISMATIC RIGHT-ANGLE WEAVE (PRAW-3)

1. Needle up your thread of choice and pick up three beads. Stitch through the first bead again to form a loop, leaving a tail at least 4 inches (10.2 cm) long **(Fig. 1)**. This is the base of the first unit.

2. Pick up three beads and stitch through the bead in the base from which your thread is emerging to form a loop. Then stitch through the next bead in the base **(Fig. 2)**. This is the first side of the unit.

3. Pick up two beads and stitch down through the nearest bead in the first side. Stitch through the bead in the base from which your thread is emerging again **(Fig. 3)**. This is the second side of the unit.

4. Stitch through the next bead in the base, then stitch up through the nearest bead in the first side added **(Fig. 4)**.

5. To create the last side, pick up one bead and stitch down through the nearest bead in the second side, then through the next bead in the base. Stitch up through the nearest bead in the first side **(Fig. 5)**.

6. To step up, stitch through the top bead of the first side **(Fig. 6)**.

7. Stitch through the three beads at the top of the unit to bring them together **(Fig. 7)**. This completes the first PRAW-3 unit. These three beads will form the base for the next unit.

8. Repeat steps 2–7 to build as many units as needed.

Fig. 1

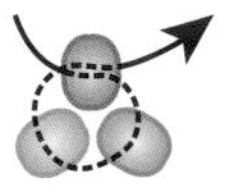

Fig. 2

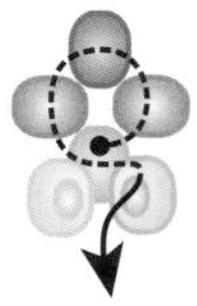

Fig. 3

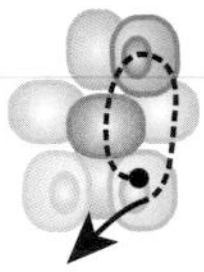

Fig. 4

Rotated 120° ➡

Fig. 5

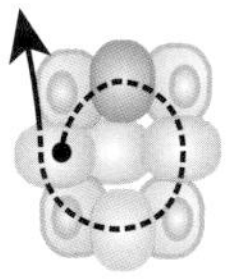

Fig. 6

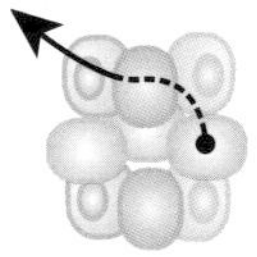

Rotated 120° ➡

Fig. 7

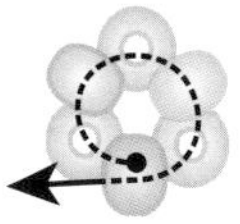

Top view

FIVE-SIDED PRISMATIC RIGHT-ANGLE WEAVE (PRAW-5)

1. Needle up your choice of thread and pick up five beads. Stitch through the first bead again to form a loop, leaving a tail at least 4 inches (10.2 cm) long **(Fig. 1)**. This is the base of the first unit.

2. Pick up three beads and stitch through the bead in the base from which your thread is emerging, then the next bead in the base **(Fig. 2)**. This is the first side of the unit.

3. Pick up two beads and stitch through the nearest bead in the first side, toward the base. Stitch through the bead in the base from which your thread is emerging, then the next bead in the base **(Fig. 3)**. This is the second side of the unit.

4. Pick up two beads and stitch down through the nearest bead on the second side, toward the base. Stitch through the bead in the base from which your thread is emerging, then the next bead in the base **(Fig. 4)**. This is the third side.

5. Pick up two beads and stitch down through the nearest bead in the third side, toward the base. Stitch through the bead in the base from which your thread is emerging **(Fig. 5)**. This is the fourth side.

6. To form the fifth side, stitch through the next bead in the base, then up through the nearest bead in the first side, in the direction away from the base. Pick up one bead and stitch down through the side bead in the fourth side. Then stitch through the bead in the base **(Fig. 6)**.

7. To step up, stitch up through the nearest bead in the first side then the top bead in the first side **(Fig. 7)**.

8. Stitch through the five beads at the top of the unit to bring them together **(Fig. 8)**. This completes the first PRAW-5 unit. These beads will form the base of the next unit.

9. Repeat steps 2–8 to build as many units as needed.

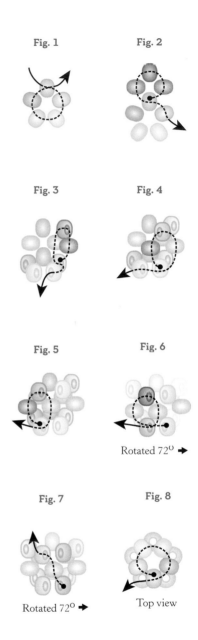

Fig. 1

Fig. 2

Fig. 3

Fig. 4

Fig. 5

Fig. 6

Rotated 72° ➡

Fig. 7

Fig. 8

Rotated 72° ➡

Top view

Small
Accessories

Bluet Earrings

Tiny, precious bluets are some of the first flowers to come out in the spring. Scattered throughout lawns in impressive numbers, these four-petaled flowers are surprisingly small, up to about half an inch (1.3 cm) wide. These earrings capture their delicate coloring, dainty beauty, and sweet simplicity. If you like the look of shorter earrings, you can choose to include only two or three flowers per earring instead of the four shown.

INSTRUCTIONS

Make Bluet A

1. Needle up one yard (91.4 cm) of thread. Pick up 1C and stitch through it again to anchor it, leaving about six inches (15.2 cm) of tail thread. You will use this as a stop bead. Pick up one rose montée and 4C **(Fig. 1)**.

2. With the rose montée facing you, stitch straight through the hole on the left of the one from which your thread is emerging **(Fig. 2)**.

3. Pick up 4C and stitch through the rose montée hole on the left of the one from which your thread is emerging **(Fig. 3)**. Repeat from the beginning of this step twice, then step up through the first 2C added **(Fig. 4)**.

Symbols

- A
- B
- C

Rose montée

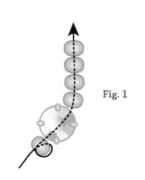
Fig. 1

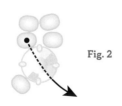
Fig. 2

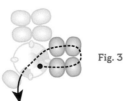
Fig. 3

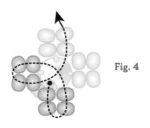
Fig. 4

SKILL LEVEL

Low intermediate

DIMENSIONS

3¹/₂ inches (8.9 cm) long from bottom to top of ear wire loop

MATERIALS

2 g stable finish galvanized champagne gold size 15º seed beads (A)

1 g pale violet-lined crystal size 15º seed beads (B)

1 g silver-lined milky Montana blue size 11º seed beads (C)

8 golden shadow crystal rose montées, SS12/PP24

2 golden shadow crystal raindrop pendants, 23 mm

2 gold-plated ear wires

Nylon beading thread

TOOLS

Beader's Tool Kit (page 2)

Size 12 beading needles

TECHNIQUES

Netting (page 8)

4. Pick up 1B and stitch through the next 2C in the group of four. Without moving your thread through the rose montée, stitch up through the first 2C in the next group of four. Repeat from the beginning three times **(Fig. 5)**. Remove the stop bead, then weave in, secure, and trim both thread ends without stitching through the rose montée again.

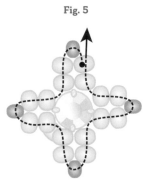

Fig. 5

Make Bluet B

5. Needle up one yard (91.4 cm) of thread. Pick up 1C to use as a stop bead and stitch through it again to anchor it, leaving about six inches (15.2 cm) of tail thread. Pick up one rose montée, 1A, 2C, and 1A **(Fig. 6, red thread)**. With the rose montée facing you, stitch straight through the hole on the left of the one from which your thread is emerging. *Pick up 1A, 2C, and 1A. Stitch through the rose montée hole on the left of the one from which your thread is emerging. Repeat from the * twice, then step up through the first A and C added **(Fig. 6, black thread)**.

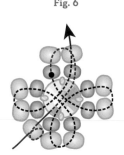

Fig. 6

6. Pick up 1C and stitch through the next C and A. Without stitching through the rose montée again, stitch through the next A and C in the next group of four. Repeat from the beginning of the step three times **(Fig. 7)**. Remove the stop bead, then weave in, secure, and trim both threads without stitching through the rose montée again.

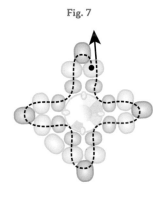

Fig. 7

Make Bluet C

7. Needle up one yard (91.4 cm) of thread. Pick up 1C to use as a stop bead and stitch through it again to anchor it, leaving about six inches (15.2 cm) of tail thread. Pick up one rose montée, 1A, 2C, 2B, 2C, and 1A **(Fig. 8, red thread)**. With the rose montée facing you, stitch straight through the hole on the left of the one from which your thread is emerging. *Pick up 1A, 2C, 2B, 2C, and 1A. Stitch through the rose montée hole on the left of the one from which your thread is emerging. Repeat from the * twice, then step up through the first A, 2C, and B added **(Fig. 8, black thread)**.

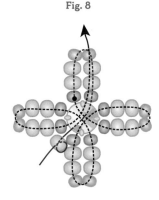

Fig. 8

8. Pick up 1B and stitch through the next B, 2C, and A. Without moving your thread through the rose montée again, stitch through the next A, two C, and B in the next group of eight beads. Repeat from the beginning of this step three times **(Fig. 9)**. Remove the stop bead, then weave in, secure, and trim both threads without stitching through the rose montée again.

9. Repeat steps 7 and 8 to make an additional Bluet C.

Assembly

10. Needle up one yard (91.4 cm) of thread. Pick up 1A to use a stop bead and stitch through it again to anchor it, leaving about six inches (15.2 cm). Pick up 8A and stitch back through the first A in the group of eight **(Fig. 10, pink thread)**. This creates the ear wire loop.

11. Attach the ear wire loop to Bluet A. Pick up 3A and working on the back side of Bluet A, stitch through the rose montée **(Fig. 10, black thread)**.

12. You will use netting to attach the remaining bluets. Working on the back side, pick up 10A and stitch through the rose montée on Bluet B. Pick up 12A and stitch through the rose montée on one of the Bluet C. Pick up 14A and stitch through the rose montée on the second Bluet C **(Fig. 11)**.

13. Pick up 13A, the crystal pendant, and 13A. Stitch through the rose montée hole that is perpendicular to the one from which your thread is emerging on the last Bluet C **(Fig. 12)**.

14. Pick up 14A and stitch diagonally through the other rose montée hole on the next Bluet C. Pick up 12A and stitch diagonally through the rose montée hole on Bluet B. Pick up 10A and stitch diagonally through the rose montée hole on Bluet A. Pick up 3A and stitch through the A below the ear wire loop **(Fig. 13, black thread)**. Stitch through the 7A in the ear wire loop, the A below the ear wire loop, then the next 3A **(Fig. 13, red thread)**.

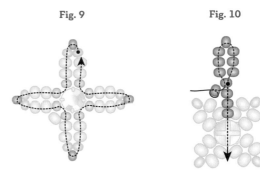

Fig. 9   Fig. 10

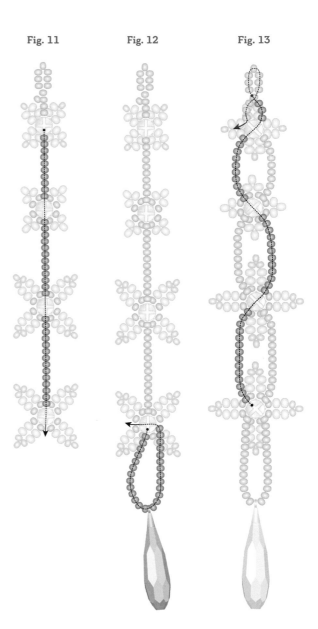

Fig. 11   Fig. 12   Fig. 13

15. Working on the back side of the rose montées, you will reinforce the netting and create a backing for each bluet. Pick up 3A and stitch through the group of 10A of the rose montée on Bluet A, on the side opposite from the one you started. Make sure the 3A stay on the back side of the earring. Pick up 3A and stitch through the next group of 12A on the side you originally started. Pick up 3A and stitch through the next group of 14A on the opposite side of the rose montée of the first Bluet C. Pick up 3A and stitch through the next group of 13A on the side you orginally started on the last Bluet C, then stitch through the pendant, and the following 13A **(Fig. 14, black thread)**.

Pick up 1A and stitch through the middle A in the next group of 3A on the back of the last Bluet C's rose montée. Pick up 1A and stitch through the next group of 14A Pick up 1A and stitch through the middle A in the group of 3A on the back of the first Bluet C's rose montée. Pick up 1A and stitch through the next group of 12A. Pick up 1A and stitch through the middle A in the group of 3A on the back side of Bluet B's rose montée. Pick up 1A and stitch through the next group of 10A. Pick up 1A and stitch through the middle A in the group of three on the back of Bluet's A rose montée. Pick up 1A and stitch through the next group of 3A, the A below the ear wire, and the next 3A **(Fig. 14, red thread)**. Repeat the thread path to reinforce it, if you can, then weave in, secure, and trim the working thread and tail thread.

16. Use pliers to attach the ear wire to the ear wire loop.

17. Repeat all steps for the second earring.

Fig. 14

Jellyfish Tassel Earrings

As a child, I saw my first jellyfish in an aquarium. I loved watching its translucent, paper-thin body undulate magically through the water. These incredible creatures continue to fascinate me today, and these earrings pay homage to some of the smaller members of this group of animals. Four MiniDuos® imitate the four-fold symmetry that many small jellyfish possess, and simple beaded fringe recreates the look of tentacles.

INSTRUCTIONS

Make the Body

1. Needle up one yard (91.4 cm) of thread and pick up 4A. Stitch through the first A again to form a loop, leaving an 8-inch (20.3 cm) tail. Stitch through all the beads again to reinforce the loop.

2. Pick up 1A and stitch through the next A in the initial loop. Repeat three times, then step up through the first A added in this round (**Fig. 1, blue thread**).

3. Pick up 3A and stitch through the next A added in the last round. Repeat three times, then step up through the first 2A added (**Fig. 1, pink thread**).

4. Pick up one MiniDuo and stitch through the middle A in the next group of 3A. Repeat three times, then step up through the first MiniDuo added in this round. Reverse direction and stitch through the outside hole of the same MiniDuo (**Fig. 1, black thread**).

Symbols

○ A

◊ MiniDuo

Fig. 1

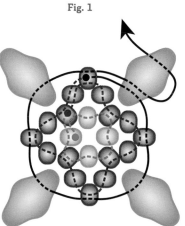

SKILL LEVEL
Low intermediate

DIMENSIONS
1¹/₂ inches (3.8 cm) long

MATERIALS
4 g nickel-plated size 15º seed beads (A)

8 Full Labrador MiniDuos

2 silver-plated ear wires

Nylon beading thread

TOOLS
Beader's Tool Kit (page 2)

Size 12 beading needles

TECHNIQUES
Netting (page 8)

Peyote stitch (page 5)

Ladder stitch (page 8)

5. Pick up 3A and stitch through the outside hole of the next MiniDuo. Repeat three times, then step up through the first 2A added this round **(Fig. 2, red thread)**. Pick up 4A and stitch through the middle A in the next group of three added in the previous row. Repeat three times; do not step up **(Fig. 2, black thread)**. Put your working thread down and leave it for attaching the fringe later.

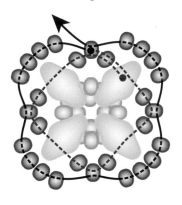

Fig. 2

Make the Fringe

6. Needle up a wingspan of thread and pick up 4A. Stitch through the first 2A again in a circular path to ladder the two pairs of A together. Stitch through the second pair again **(Fig. 3, pink thread)**. This will make a grid that will house the individual fringes that you make in the later steps.

Fig. 3

7. Pick up 2A and stitch through the last pair of A, then stitch through the newly added pair again **(Fig. 3, blue thread)**. Repeat twice to add two more pairs of A **(Fig. 3, black thread)**.

8. Fold the last two pairs of A over so they overlap the second and third pairs. Ladder the fifth pair of A to the second pair of A in the laddered sequence **(Fig. 4)**.

Fig. 4

9. Ladder a new pair of A **(Fig. 5)**. Ladder this new pair of A to the first pair of A in the laddered sequence **(Fig. 6)**.

Fig. 5

10. Ladder two more pairs of A **(Fig. 7)**. Fold the last two pairs of A over so they overlap the fifth and sixth pairs of the laddered sequence. Ladder the eighth pair of A to the fifth pair of A in the laddered sequence **(Fig. 8)**. Ladder a new pair of A and then ladder them to the fourth pair of A in the laddered sequence. Weave in the tail thread by stitching back and forth along the threads on the top of the grid.

Fig. 6

Fig. 7

Fig. 8

JELLYFISH TASSEL EARRINGS — 23

11. To make one fringe, pick up 30A, skip the last A, and stitch back through the other 29A. Stitch up into the pair of A from which your thread emerges, then down through the next pair of laddered A **(Fig. 9)**. Leave a little slack in the thread to allow the fringe to dangle.

12. Repeat step 11 eight more times, adding one fringe to each of the laddered pairs of As in the grid. When you're finished, weave in, secure, and trim your working thread.

Assembly

13. Return to the working thread on the body. To attach the laddered grid to the body, stitch through the thread between the beads at one of the corners of the grid; do not stitch through any beads. Stitch through the same A from which your working thread was first emerging, then through the next group of 4A on the body and the middle A in the next group of 3A **(Fig. 10)**. Pull tightly to cinch the corner of the grid up into the jellyfish body.

14. Repeat step 13 three more times to attach the other three corners of the tentacle grid. Make sure that the tentacle grid is nestled inside the edges of the body. Once the grid is attached, weave in, secure, and trim your working thread.

15. Create the loop that you'll use to attach the ear wire. Needle up the tail thread on the top of the body. Pick up 7A and stitch through the A directly across the one from which your thread emerged **(Fig. 11)**.

16. Stitch back through the 7A just added and the first A in the body. Repeat the thread path at least once more to reinforce, then weave in, secure, and trim the thread. Attach the ear wire to this top loop.

17. Repeat steps 1–16 for the second earring.

Fig. 9

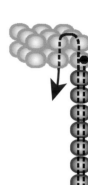

Fig. 10

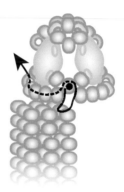

Fig. 11

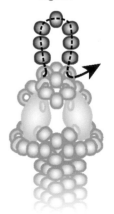

« Tip: *To make a necklace instead of earrings, create one jellyfish tassel as described, then attach it to a chain or beaded rope using a jump ring.*

⋎ Variation: *Use crystal AB size 15° seed beads for A and turqouise blue Picasso Czech MiniDuos.*

Leaf Hair Ornament

Where I live, there are many native bushes that produce berries. This hair accessory is inspired by the welcome sight of berries gathered within a small cluster of leaves. The piece would make a sweet, elegant accent to either a casual cascade of curls or a formal updo. The right-angle weave base for the leaves and berries can be adapted to fit around different sized hair accessories.

INSTRUCTIONS

Make the Base

1. Needle up a wingspan of thread and work a row of right-angle weave (RAW) with six units; each unit is made from 4A. Work four more rows, still using 4A for each RAW unit, for a total of five rows. This strip of flat right-angle weave will form the base. To keep your beadwork tight and even, reinforce the thread path after completing each RAW unit.

2. Wrap the strip of RAW around the headband, aligning the last (fifth) row with the first. With the thread emerging from the last bead on the end of the fifth row, pick up 1A, and stitch through the corresponding A in the first row. Pick up 1A and stitch through the A in the fifth row again in a circular fashion to create a RAW unit. Step up through the last A added in this step **(Fig. 1, pink thread)**.

3. Stitch through the next A in the fifth row. Pick up 1A and stitch through the corresponding A on the first row. Stitch through the A added in step 2, then step up through to the A just added. Repeat from the beginning of the step four times to finish zipping the first and last rows together **(Fig. 1, black thread)**.

SKILL LEVEL
Intermediate

DIMENSIONS
1¹/2 inches (3.8 cm) in diameter

MATERIALS
3 g sterling silver-plated size 15º seed beads (A)

3 iridescent dove gray crystal pearls, 3 mm

3 iridescent dove gray crystal pearls, 4 mm

1 silver-plated headband finding, 3 mm

Crystal braided fishing line thread, 4 lb or 6 lb

TOOLS
Beader's Tool Kit (page 2)

Size 12 beading needles

TECHNIQUES
Right-angle weave (RAW) (page 10)

Netting (page 8)

Symbols

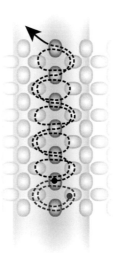

A

3-mm pearl

4-mm pearl

Fig. 1

Make the Leaves

4. Work your way to the other side of the join by stitching through the next 2A in the last RAW unit you created.

5. Pick up 1A and stitch through the next 2A in the next RAW unit down. Repeat three times to add a total of 4A **(Fig. 2, blue thread)**. You will use these beads to attach four of the five leaves.

   Note: The RAW beads stitched in this step and the next are outlined in pink in Fig. 2 for clarity.

6. Weave back up the RAW strip to the bead where you began step 4 **(Fig. 2, black thread)**.

Leaf A

7. Work one row of RAW that is nine units long, with 4A in each unit. This row forms the center of the leaf.

8. Stitch through the next A in the last unit so your thread is heading toward the start of the RAW row **(Fig. 3, pink thread)**.

9. Pick up 20A and stitch through the bottom 3A in the first RAW unit worked in step 7. Pick up 20A and stitch through the A on the side of the last (ninth) RAW unit of the leaf center. Skip the A at the top of the unit and stitch through the following A, then pass through the first A of the first added group of 20A **(Fig. 3, black thread)**. You now have your leaf outline and will proceed to fill in the veins.

10. Pick up 2A and stitch through the bottom 3A in the third RAW unit from the tip of the leaf center. Pick up 2A, and moving toward the base, stitch through the second, third, and fourth A in the group of 20A on the other side of the leaf outline **(Fig. 4, pink thread)**.

11. Pick up 3A and stitch through the bottom 3A in the fourth RAW unit from the tip of the leaf center. Pick up 3A, and moving toward the base, stitch through the fifth and sixth A in the group of 20A on the first side of the leaf outline **(Fig. 4, tan thread)**.

12. Pick up 4A and stitch through the bottom 3A in the fifth RAW unit from the tip of the leaf center. Pick up 4A, and moving

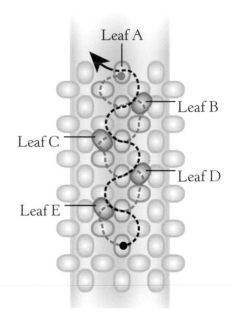

Fig. 2

Fig. 3

toward the base, stitch through the seventh and eighth A in the group of 20A on the other side of the leaf outline **(Fig. 4, purple thread)**.

13. Pick up 5A and stitch through the bottom 3A in the sixth RAW unit from the tip of the leaf center. Pick up 5A, and moving toward the base, stitch through the ninth and tenth A in the group of 20A on the first side of the leaf outline **(Fig. 4, blue thread)**.

14. Pick up 6A and stitch through the bottom 3A in the seventh RAW unit down from the tip of the leaf center. Pick up 6A, and moving toward the base, stitch through the 11th and 12th A in the group of 20A on the other side of the leaf outline **(Fig. 4, green thread)**.

15. Pick up 6A and stitch through the bottom 3A in the eighth RAW unit down from the tip of the leaf center. Pick up 6A, and moving toward the base, stitch through the 13th to 20th A in the group of 20A on the first side of the leaf outline **(Fig. 4, brown thread)**.

16. Stitch through the next A down in the RAW base, the A after it in the same RAW unit and the first of the additional 4A added to the base **(Fig. 4, black thread)**.

Leaf B

17. Create Leaf B using the same technique outlined in steps 7–16. Make the center of Leaf B seven RAW units long, and use 17A for each side of the leaf to create the outline. The thread path and the number of A needed to make the veins are shown in **Figure 5 (blue thread)**.

18. When your thread is emerging from the last A on one side of the leaf, stitch through the next A in the first RAW unit of the leaf center, the first extra A added to the RAW base, the next 2A in the same RAW unit, and the next extra A **(Fig. 5, black thread)**.

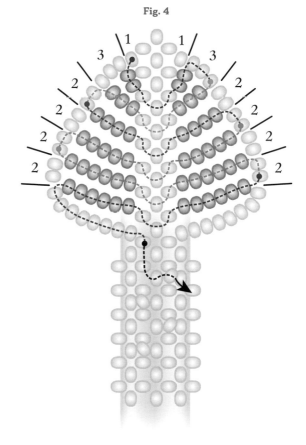

Fig. 4

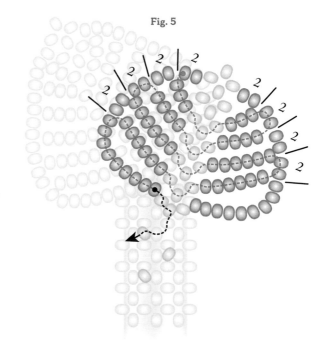

Fig. 5

Leaf C

19. Create Leaf C using the same technique outlined in steps 7–16. Make the center of Leaf C six RAW units long, and use 14A for each side of the leaf outline. The thread path and the number of A needed to make the veins are shown in **Figure 6 (pink thread)**.

20. When your thread is emerging from the last A on one side of the leaf outline, stitch through the next A in the first RAW unit of the leaf center, the extra A added to the RAW base, the next 2A, and the next extra A **(Fig. 6, black thread)**.

Leaf D

21. Create Leaf D using the same technique outlined in steps 7–16. Make the center of Leaf D five RAW units long, and use 11A for each side of the leaf outline. The thread path and the number of A needed to make the veins are shown in **Figure 7**.

22. When your thread is emerging from the last A on one side of the leaf outline, stitch through the next A in the first RAW unit added, then the extra A added to the RAW base, the next 2A, and the last extra A **(Fig. 7)**.

Leaf E

23. Create Leaf E using the same technique outlined in steps 7–16. Make the center of Leaf E four RAW units long, and use 8A on each side of the leaf outline. The thread path and the number of A needed to make the veins are shown in **Figure 8**.

24. When your thread is emerging from the last A on one side of the leaf, stitch through the next A in the first RAW unit added, the extra A added to the RAW base, and the next A in the RAW base **(Fig. 8)**.

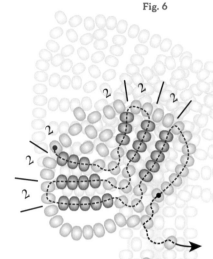

Fig. 6

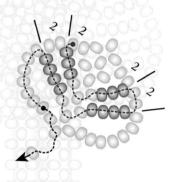

Fig. 7

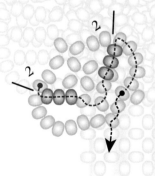

Fig. 8

Fig. 9

Make the Berries

25. The five berries are made with pearls and added to the base in the same row of RAW units that was used to work the leaves. Pick up one 4-mm pearl and 1A. Stitch back through the pearl and the side A in the next RAW unit down, which should be the last unit on the edge of the base. Stitch through the next A in the same unit. Pick up one 3-mm pearl and 1A. Stitch back through the pearl and the next A in the same unit, toward Leaf A. Pick up one 4-mm pearl and 1A. Stitch back through the pearl and the A in the next unit up, moving toward Leaf A. Pick up one 4-mm pearl and 1A. Stitch back through the pearl and the next A in the same unit, then the A after that. Pick up one 3-mm pearl and 1A. Stitch back through the pearl and through the next A in the same RAW unit. Working toward Leaf A, stitch through the next A. Pick up one 3-mm pearl and 1A. Stitch back through the pearl and the A that is on the opposite side of the next RAW unit up in the base **(Fig. 9)**. Weave in, secure, and trim your thread.

Note: In Figure 9, the leaves are not shown for clarity, and the added A are outlined in blue.

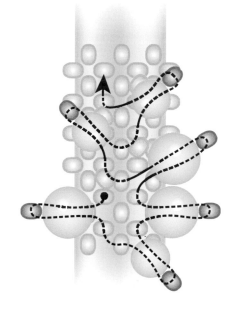

« Variation: *For a gold version of the hair ornament, use 24-karat gold-plated size 15° seed beads for A and 3-mm and 4-mm creamrose light pearls. For the base of the ornament, work three rows of flat RAW in step 1 with six units in each row, then zip the strip around a bobby pin. To fit the strip around another type of armature, work the RAW units in step 1 and compare the width of the strip to the circumference of the armature as you work. Keep in mind that the zipping process will add between 1 and 2 mm to the width of the strip. You can also zip the beadwork around a sturdy hair elastic if it is wide enough. Avoid using thinner elastics, which will stress the zipped RAW strip and eventually cause the beads to break.*

Little Lilies Ring

There are many types of wild lilies in various parts of the world. These blossoms come in many different shapes and sizes and in a full spectrum of colors and markings as well. This fanciful ring is a playful interpretation of three small lily flowers gathered into a mini bouquet. The petals, which surround a bezeled stone, are made with a combination of simple techniques and sewn onto a peyote-stitched ring band.

TOOLS

Beader's Tool Kit (page 2)

Size 12 beading needles

TECHNIQUES

Odd-count peyote stitch (page 6)

Even-count peyote stitch (page 6)

Netting (page 8)

Right-angle weave (RAW) (page 10)

Symbols

☐ A   ⬭ C
● B   ◌ K

INSTRUCTIONS

Make the Flowers

Pink Flower

1. Needle up a wingspan of thread and pick up 12A. Stitch through the first 4A again to form a loop **(Fig. 1, pink thread)**. Leave a tail thread just long enough to weave into the beadwork later and secure.

2. You will start by making the bezel for the center of the flower. Pick up 1A and stitch through the next 4A in the loop. Repeat twice, then step up through the first A added in this step **(Fig. 1, blue thread)**.

3. Pick up 6A and stitch through the next A in the previous round. Repeat twice, then step up through the first 3A in the first group of 6A added in this round **(Fig. 1, black thread)**.

Fig. 1

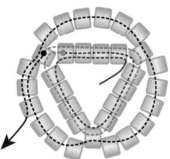

SKILL LEVEL

Intermediate

DIMENSIONS

1¹/₂ inches (3.81 cm) tall and
1¹/₂ inches (3.81 cm) wide

MATERIALS

PINK FLOWER

1 g fuschia-lined crystal AB size 11⁰ cylinder beads (A)

1 g permanent pink opal silver-lined size 15⁰ seed beads (B)

1 g dyed silver-lined Paris pink size 11⁰ seed beads (C)

BLUE FLOWER

1 g dyed semi-frosted silver-lined aqua size 11⁰ cylinder beads (D)

1 g dyed stable finish silver-lined aqua size 15⁰ seed beads (E)

1 g sparkling sky blue-lined crystal AB size 11⁰ seed beads (F)

GREEN FLOWER AND RING BAND

2 g dyed aqua green silver-lined alabaster size 11⁰ cylinder beads (G)

1 g dyed sea green silver-lined alabaster size 15⁰ seed beads (H)

1 g stable finish galvanized green teal size 11⁰ seed beads (J)

1 g gilt-lined white opal size 15⁰ seed beads (K)

3 crystal trilliant fancy stones, 7 mm

Crystal braided fishing line thread, 6 lb

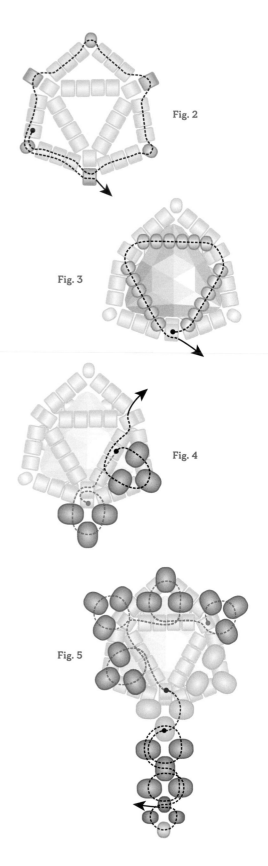

4. Pick up 1B and stitch through the next 3A in the same group of 6A. Pick up 1A, skip the next A (added in step 2), and stitch through the first 3A in the next group of 6A. Repeat from the beginning of this step twice, then step up through the first A added in this round. Stitch through the next 3A in the previous round and the A added this round **(Fig. 2)**.

Fig. 2

5. Pick up 6K and stitch through the next A added in the previous round. Repeat twice; do not step up. Place one 7-mm trilliant stone, inserting each corner of the stone underneath a group of 6K **(Fig. 3)**. Pull your thread tightly after the stone is in place. If the groups of 6K are too loose to hold the corners of the stone in place, you may have to undo the round and remove one K from each group. Alternatively, you can try repeating the thread path through the groups of 6K multiple times to secure the stone.

Fig. 3

6. Turn the beadwork over to the back. Stitch through the adjacent A above the one from which your thread is emerging. *Pick up 3C and stitch through the same A again in a circular fashion. Stitch through the next 3A added in step 1 **(Fig. 4, blue thread)**.

7. Pick up 3C and stitch through the second and third bead in the group of 4A added in step 1. Stitch through the fourth A in the same group and the next A at the corner of the bezel **(Fig. 4, black thread)**.

Fig. 4

8. Repeat step 6 from the * and step 7 twice **(Fig. 5, blue thread)**.

9. Stitch through the first 2C in the first group of 3C added in step 6 **(Fig. 5, pink thread)**.

10. Pick up 3C and stitch in a circular fashion through the C at which you started this step to form a RAW unit. Stitch through the first 2C just added in this step. Pick up 1C, 1B, and 1C. Stitch through the C at the end of the last RAW unit to form another RAW unit, then stitch through the first C and B just added. Pick up 1B, 1K, and 1B and stitch through the B in the previous unit again to form another RAW unit **(Fig. 5, black thread)**. These RAW units form the base for the first petal.

Fig. 5

Fig. 6

11. Stitch down through the three previous RAW units. Pick up 1C and stitch through the first 2C in the next group of 3C in the bezel **(Fig. 6)**.

12. Repeat steps 10 and 11 five times to form the base for five more petals. After adding the last single C, stitch through the next 2C in the bottom RAW unit in the next petal base, then through the next single C between this petal base and the following one **(Fig. 7, blue thread)**. Note that you are now working in the opposite direction around the bezel.

13. Pick up 2C and 4B and stitch through the nearest B on the top RAW unit in the petal base. Skip the K and stitch through the next B in the same RAW unit. Pick up 4B and 2C and stitch through the next single C between this petal base and the following one **(Fig. 7, black thread)**.

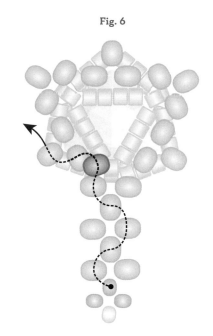

14. Repeat step 13 five more times to complete the remaining five petals. If any of the petals do not appear concave when viewing the flower from the front, simply push in the RAW petal bases and pull out the lines of B and C added to the front of the petal. When you've completed all the petals, leave your working thread hanging from a single C between petals on the back side for assembly. Weave in, secure, and trim your tail thread.

Blue Flower

15. To create the blue lily, repeat steps 1–14 using the blue seed beads: use D in place of A, E in place of B, and F in place of C. Use K as directed.

Green Flower

16. To create the green lily, repeat steps 1–14 using the green seed beads: use G in place of A, H in place of B, and J in place of C. Use K as directed.

Fig. 7

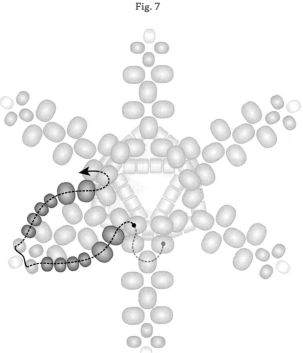

Make the Ring Band

17. Needle up a wingspan of thread and pick up 13G. Leave a tail thread just long enough to weave into the beadwork later and secure. Create a strip of odd-count peyote stitch 25 rows long. This is the base onto which you will sew your lily flowers.

Dahlia Brooch

There are few things more stunning than the array of innumerable tiny, curved petals that makes up a dahlia. Each petal is a perfect display of color blending, and the shape of the individual petals and the number of petals per flower can vary from blossom to blossom. This dahlia brooch combines my favorite qualities of these blooms: tiny, sculpted petals that gradually decrease in size and a dramatic color gradient in each petal.

INSTRUCTIONS

You will assemble the dahlia by creating seven petal rings, each of which has six petals. The rings are constructed separately and then stitched together so that the petals of each ring fall between the petals of the previous ring. You will start with the largest petal rings first. The assembled petal rings are stacked in descending order, with the largest on the bottom and smallest on the top.

Make Petal Ring 1

1. Needle up a wingspan of thread and pick up 36A. Stitch through the first three beads again to form a loop. Do not tie a knot. Leave a tail thread just long enough to weave into the beadwork later and trim. Hold onto the tail until you've completed the first round to keep the thread tension tight.

2. Pick up 5A, 1B, 1C, and 1D **(Fig. 1, blue thread)**. Working back toward the ring of A, peyote stitch 1D, 1B, and 2A individually. Stitch through the next 6A in the ring **(Fig. 1, black thread)**. This is the base of the first petal.

Symbols

- ▢ A   ◉ E
- ▢ B   ◉ F
- ▢ C   ◯ G
- ▢ D

Fig. 1

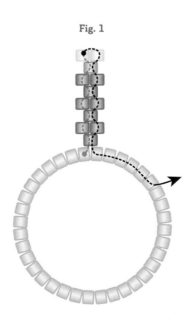

SKILL LEVEL

Intermediate

DIMENSIONS

1¹/₂ inches (3.8 cm) diameter and ¹/₂ inch (1.3 cm) high

MATERIALS

3 g luminous jazzberry size 11⁰ cylinder beads (A)

3 g salmon ceylon size 11⁰ cylinder beads (B)

1 g luminous creamsicle size 11⁰ cylinder beads (C)

1 g luminous sun glow size 11⁰ cylinder beads (D)

1 g ceylon peach cobbler size 15⁰ seed beads (E)

1 g light daffodil ceylon size 15⁰ seed beads (F)

2 g light lemon ice ceylon size 15⁰ seed beads (G)

1 three-hole brooch finding, 1 inch (2.5 cm)

Crystal braided fishing line thread, 4 lb or 6 lb

TOOLS

Beader's Tool Kit (page 2)

Size 12 beading needles

TECHNIQUES

Peyote stitch (page 5)

Netting (page 8)

Ladder stitch (page 8)

3. Repeat step 2 five more times to create a total of six petal bases **(Fig. 2, blue thread)**. After adding the sixth petal base, stitch through one more A in the ring so the thread is emerging from the bead after the one at which you started this round **(Fig. 2, black thread)**.

4. Working toward the tip of the petal base, peyote stitch 2A, 1B, and 1D individually. Pick up 3G and stitch through the adjacent D. Peyote stitch 1D, 1B, and 2A individually. Stitch through the 2A in the section of the ring under the petal **(Fig. 3, blue thread)**. Step up through the first A added **(Fig. 3, black thread)**.

5. Peyote stitch 2B, 1D, and 1G individually. Pass through the 3G at the tip of the petal. Peyote stitch 1G, 1D, and 2B individually, then stitch through the 2A in the section of the ring under the petal **(Fig. 4, blue thread)**. Step up through the first B added in this round **(Fig. 4, black thread)**.

6. Peyote stitch 1B, 1D, and 1G individually. Pass through the 5G at the tip of the petal. Pull tightly so that the petal curves toward you, and remove as much slack from the thread as possible. Peyote stitch 1G, 1D, 1B individually. Stitch through the next A in the petal, the 2A in the section of the ring beneath the petal, and the following A on the other side of the petal **(Fig. 5, blue thread)**. Step up through the next 2B **(Fig. 5, black thread)**.

7. Pick up 4G and stitch through the 7G at the tip of the petal, pulling tightly so that the new beads move to the front side of the rounded petal. Pick up 4G and stitch through the next 2B and A in the petal, and the 2A in the section of the ring beneath the petal **(Fig. 6, blue thread)**. Stitch through the next 6A in the initial ring so that your thread emerges from the second A in the pair of A just beneath the next petal base **(Fig. 6, black thread)**.

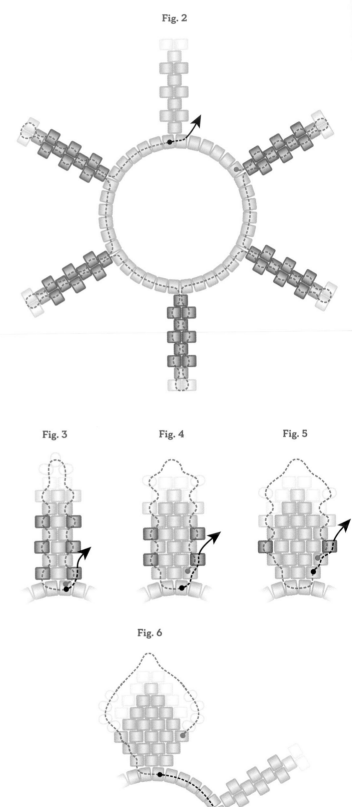

Fig. 2

Fig. 3 Fig. 4 Fig. 5

Fig. 6

8. Repeat steps 4–7 five times to complete the five remaining petals in the ring. Leave your working thread hanging for assembly, but weave in, secure, and trim your tail thread.

Make Petal Ring 2

9. Petal Ring 2 is the same size as Petal Ring 1, but its petals feature a different color pattern. To begin, repeat step 1 to create a ring using 36A.

10. Pick up 2A, 4B, 1C, and 1D. Working back toward the ring of A, peyote stitch 1D, 2B, and 1A individually. Stitch through the next 6A in the ring. This is the base of the first petal.

11. Repeat step 10 five more times to create a total of six petal bases. After adding the sixth petal base, stitch through one more A in the ring so the thread is emerging from the bead after the one at which you started this round.

12. Working toward the tip of the petal base, peyote stitch 1A, 1B, 1C, and 1D individually. Pick up 3G and stitch through the adjacent D. Peyote stitch 1D, 1C, 1B, and 1A individually. Stitch through the 2A in the section of the ring beneath the petal, then step up through the first A added in this round **(Fig. 7, blue thread)**.

13. Peyote stitch 1B, 1C, 1D, and 1G individually, then pass through all 3G on the tip of the petal. Peyote stitch 1G, 1D, 1C, and 1B individually. Stitch through the 2A in the section of the ring beneath the petal, then step up through the next A and B in the petal **(Fig. 7, black thread)**.

14. Peyote stitch 1C, 1D, and 1G individually. Pass through all 5G at the tip of the petal. Pull tightly to curve the petal toward you. Peyote stitch 1G, 1D, and 1C individually, then stitch through the next A in the petal, the 2A in the section of the ring beneath the petal, and next A and B in the petal. Step up through the next C **(Fig. 8, blue thread)**.

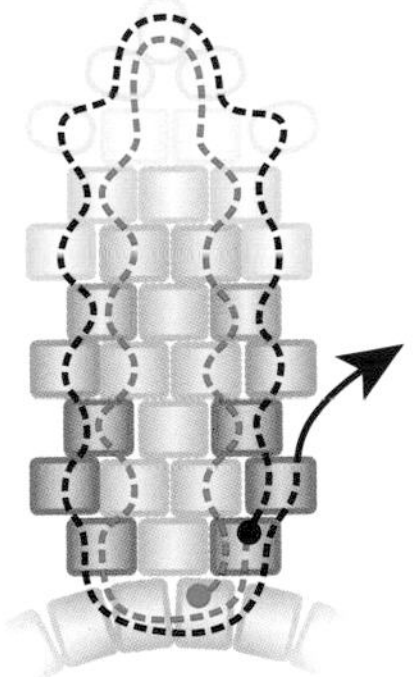

15. Pick up 4G and stitch through the 7G at the tip of the petal, pulling tightly so that the new beads move to the front side of the rounded petal. Pick up 4G and stitch through the next C, next B, and next A in the petal, and the 2A in the section of the ring beneath the petal **(Fig. 8, pink thread)**. Stitch through the next 6A in the ring so that your thread emerges from the second A in the pair of A just beneath the next petal base **(Fig. 8, black thread)**.

16. Repeat steps 12–15 five more times to complete the five remaining petals in the ring. Leave your working thread hanging for assembly, but weave in, secure, and trim your tail thread.

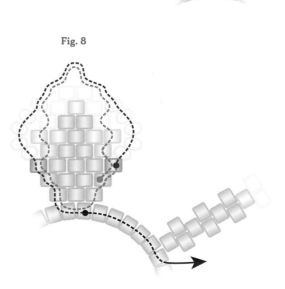

Fig. 7

Fig. 8

Make Petal Ring 3

17. To begin Petal Ring 3, repeat step 1, but use 30A to form the initial ring.

18. Pick up 2A, 3B, 1C, and 1D **(Fig. 9, blue thread)**. Working back toward the ring of A, peyote stitch 1D, 2B, and 1A individually. Stitch through the A from which your thread started, then the next 5A (6A in total) **(Fig. 9, black thread)**. This is the base of the first petal.

19. Repeat step 18 five more times to create a total of six petal bases. Then stitch up through the first A added in the first petal base.

20. Peyote stitch 1B, 1C, and 1D individually. Pick up 3G and stitch through the adjacent D. Peyote stitch 1D, 1C, and 1B individually. Stitch through the single A beneath the petal and step up through the next A and B in the petal **(Fig. 10, blue thread)**.

21. Peyote stitch 1C, 1D, and 1G individually. Pass through the 3B at the tip of the petal. Peyote stitch 1G, 1D, and 1C individually. Then stitch through the next A in the petal and the single A beneath the petal. Step up through the next A, B, and C **(Fig. 10, black thread)**.

22. Pick up 4G and stitch through the 5G at the tip of the petal, pulling tightly so that the new beads move to the front side of the rounded petal. Pick up 4G and stitch through the next C, B, and A in the petal, and the single A in the section of the ring beneath the petal **(Fig. 11, blue thread)**. Stitch through the next 5A in the ring and the first A in the next petal base **(Fig. 11, black thread)**.

23. Repeat steps 20–22 five more times to create a total of six petals. Leave your working thread hanging for assembly, but weave in, secure, and trim your tail thread.

Make Petal Ring 4

24. To begin Petal Ring 4, repeat step 1, but use 24As to form the initial ring.

25. Pick up 1A, 2B, 1C, and 1D. Working back toward the ring of A, peyote stitch 1D, 1B, and 1A individually. Stitch through the next A in the ring **(Fig. 12, blue thread)**, then the next 3A (4A total) **(Fig. 12, black thread)**. This is the first petal base.

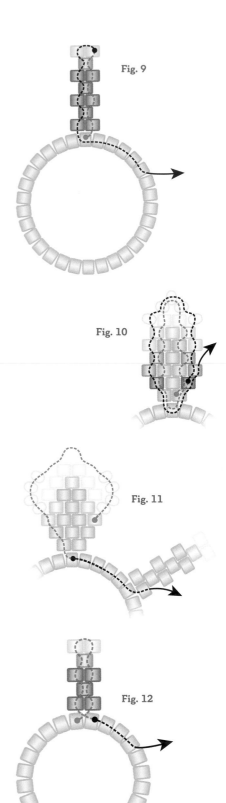

Fig. 9

Fig. 10

Fig. 11

Fig. 12

26. Repeat step 25 five more times to create a total of six petal bases. Then stitch through the first A added in the first petal base.

27. Peyote stitch 1B and 1D individually. Pick up 3G and stitch through the adjacent D. Peyote stitch 1D and 1B individually. Reverse direction and stitch through the adjacent A and next B in the petal **(Fig. 13, pink thread)**.

28. Pick up 4F, and stitch through the 3G at the tip of the petal. Pick up 4F and stitch through the next B and A in the petal, and the next A in the initial ring **(Fig. 13, blue thread)**. Stitch through the next 3A in the ring and the first A in the next petal base **(Fig. 13, black thread)**.

29. Repeat steps 27–28 five more times to create a total of six petals. Leave your working thread hanging for assembly, but weave in, secure, and trim your tail thread.

Make Petal Ring 5

30. To begin Petal Ring 5, repeat step 1, but use 18A to form the initial ring.

31. Pick up 1A, 1B, 1C, and 1D. Working back toward the ring of A, peyote stitch 1D and 1B individually. Stitch through the next A in the ring **(Fig. 14, blue thread)**, then the next 2A (3A total) **(Fig. 14, black thread)**. This is the first petal base.

32. Repeat step 31 five more times to create a total of six petal bases. Then stitch through one more A in the initial ring.

33. Pick up 1B and stitch through the next B in the petal base. Make one peyote stitch with 1D. Pick up 3F and stitch through the adjacent D. Make one peyote stitch with 1D. Pick up 1B and stitch through the pair of A in the section of the ring under the petal. Step up through the first B added in this round **(Fig. 15, pink thread)**.

34. Pick up 4F and stitch through the 3F at the tip of the petal. Pick up 4F and stitch through the next B, then the pair of A in the section of the ring under the petal **(Fig. 15, blue thread)**. Stitch through the next 3A in the ring **(Fig. 15, black thread)**.

35. Repeat steps 33–34 five more times to create a total of six petals. Leave your working thread hanging for assembly, but weave in, secure, and trim your tail thread.

Fig. 13

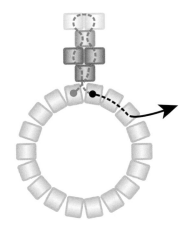

Fig. 14

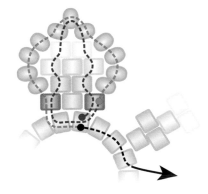

Fig. 15

Make Petal Ring 6

36. To begin Petal Ring 6, repeat step 1, but use 12A to form the initial ring.

37. Pick up 1A, 1B, 1C, and 3F. Stitch back through the C and B. Pick up 1A and stitch through the A in the initial ring at which you started this step. Stitch through the next 2A in the ring **(Fig. 16)**. This is the first petal base.

38. Repeat step 37 five more times to create a total of six petal bases. Then stitch up through the first A in the first petal base.

39. Pick up 2E and stitch through the 3F on the tip of the petal. Pick up 2E and stitch through the next A and the single A beneath the petal **(Fig. 17, blue thread)**. Stitch through the next 2A in the ring, then stitch through the first A in the next petal base **(Fig. 17, black thread)**.

40. Repeat step 39 five more times to create a total of six petals. Leave your working thread hanging for assembly, but weave in, secure, and trim your tail thread.

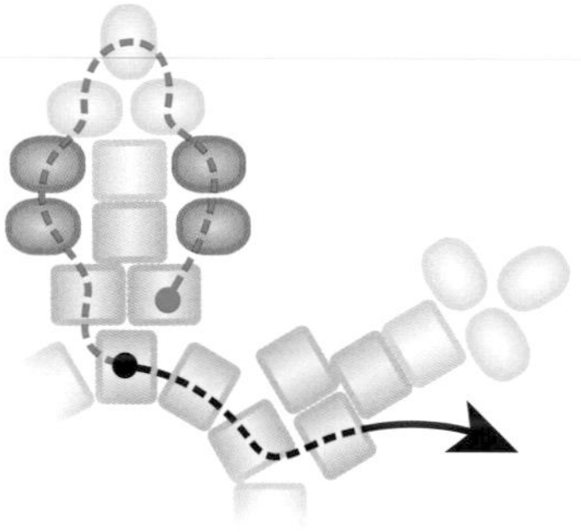

Make Petal Ring 7

41. Needle up one yard of thread and pick up 6A. Stitch through all the beads again to form a loop, then stitch through one or two more, leaving a tail thread just long enough to weave into the beadwork later. You will create two layers of petals using this ring of A.

Bottom Petal Layer

42. Pick up 1A, 1B, 3E, 1B, and 1A. Stitch through the same A at which you started this round and the next A in the ring **(Fig. 18, blue thread)**.

43. Pick up 1A, 1B, 3E, and 1B. Stitch back through the nearest A in the previous petal, the A in the initial ring, and the next A in the initial ring **(Fig. 18, pink thread)**. Repeat from the beginning of this step four more times to create a total of six petals. Do not step up **(Fig. 18, black thread)**.

Fig. 16

Fig. 17

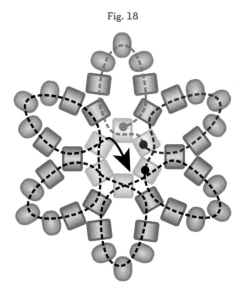

Fig. 18

Top Petal Layer

44. Pick up 5F and stitch through the next A in the initial ring **(Fig. 19, blue thread)**. Repeat from the beginning of this step five more times for a total of six petals **(Fig. 19, black thread)**. Leave your thread hanging for assembly, but weave in, secure, and trim your tail thread.

Assembly

45. Center Petal Ring 2 on top of Petal Ring 1; the petals of Petal Ring 2 should fall between those of Petal Ring 1. Needle up the hanging thread on Petal Ring 2. You will ladder together the following bead pairs: the 2A under each petal of Petal Ring 1 to the 2A centered between each petal of Petal Ring 2 **(Fig. 20, blue Xs)** and the 2A centered between each petal of Petal Ring 1 to the 2A under each petal of Petal Ring 2 **(Fig. 20, black Xs)**. Refer to **Figure 21** for an example of a thread path that you will use to ladder the pairs together. Weave in, secure, and trim the thread after laddering all twelve bead pairs.

Tip: It can be helpful to switch to a short, sharp needle to pass through the beads in this step, especially when you reach the end of the stitching. Don't be afraid to really push and pull the petals around to access tough-to-reach places as you stitch the rings together. Don't worry too much if you can't complete every single stitch in this step, as some can be very hard to reach once the petals are well sewn together. All that really matters is that the petals are held in place in an alternating fashion to mimic the look of a real dahlia flower.

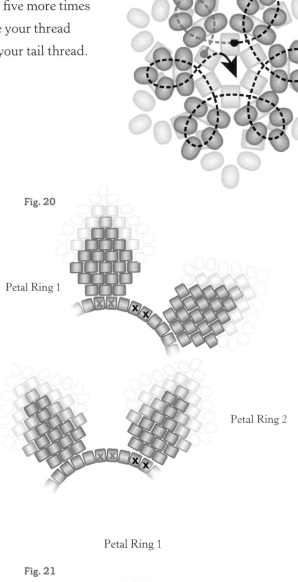

Fig. 19

Fig. 20

Petal Ring 1

Petal Ring 2

Petal Ring 1

Fig. 21

Petal Ring 2

46. Center Petal Ring 3 on top of Petal Ring 2; the petals of Petal Ring 3 should fall between those of Petal Ring 2. Needle up the hanging thread on Petal Ring 3. Ladder the 2A centered between the petals of Petal Ring 2 to the bottom 2A in each petal of Petal Ring 3 **(Fig. 22, blue Xs)**. Weave in, secure, and trim your thread.

47. Center Petal Ring 4 on top of Petal Ring 3; the petals of Petal Ring 4 should fall between those of Petal Ring 3. Needle up the hanging thread on Petal Ring 4. Ladder the 2A centered under each petal of Petal Ring 4 to the 2A centered between each petal of Petal Ring 3 **(Fig. 23, blue Xs)**. Weave in, secure, and trim your thread.

48. Center Petal Ring 5 on top of Petal Ring 4; the petals of Petal Ring 5 should fall between those of Petal Ring 4. Needle up the hanging thread on Petal Ring 5. Ladder the 2A centered under each petal of Petal Ring 5 to the 2A centered between each petal of Petal Ring 4 **(Fig. 24, blue Xs)**. Weave in, secure, and trim your thread.

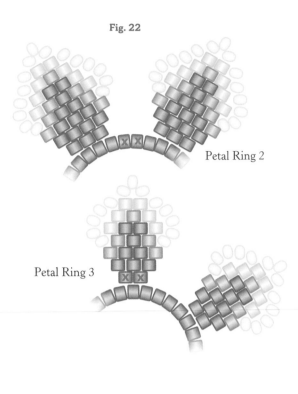

Fig. 22

Petal Ring 2

Petal Ring 3

49. Place Petal Ring 6 centered on top of Petal Ring 5; the petals of Petal Ring 6 should fall between those of Petal Ring 5. Needle up the hanging thread on Petal Ring 6. Ladder the single A centered under each petal of Petal Ring 6 to the single A centered between each petal of Petal Ring 5 **(Fig. 25, blue Xs)**. Weave in, secure, and trim your thread.

50. Place Petal Ring 7 centered on top of Petal Ring 6; the petals in the bottom layer of Petal Ring 7 should fall between the petals of Petal Ring 6. Needle up the hanging thread on Petal Ring 7. Ladder each A in the initial ring on Petal Ring 7 to the single A centered between each petal of Petal Ring 6 **(Fig. 26, blue Xs)**. Weave in, secure, and trim your thread.

51. Needle up an additional 18 inches (45.7 cm) of thread on the back side of Petal Ring 1 or use hanging thread if you still have enough remaining. Bring it through to a pair of As in the initial ring, centered between two petals. String on one of the end holes of the brooch finding, moving from the back side of the finding to front. Pick up 5G and stitch through the same 2A in the initial ring again **(Fig. 27, blue thread)**. Retrace the thread path at least once to reinforce. Stitch through the next 18A in the initial ring **(Fig. 27, pink thread)**. String on the opposite hole of the brooch finding, moving from the back side of the finding to front. Pick up 5B and stitch through the last 2A in the initial ring again **(Fig. 27, black thread)**. Retrace the thread path at least once to reinforce, then weave in, secure, and trim your thread.

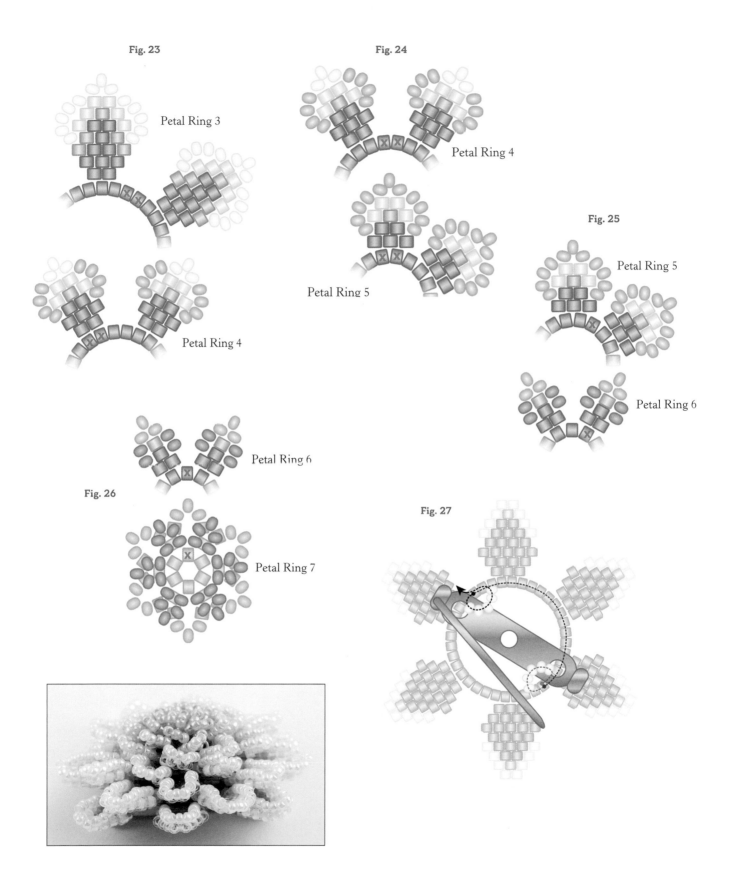

Fig. 23

Petal Ring 3

Petal Ring 4

Fig. 24

Petal Ring 4

Petal Ring 5

Fig. 25

Petal Ring 5

Petal Ring 6

Fig. 26

Petal Ring 6

Petal Ring 7

Fig. 27

Raindrop Anklet

If you catch the aftermath of a rainfall, when the clouds begin to clear, you'll notice how the light from the sky reflects off the fallen water droplets and makes them shimmer like tiny jewels. The sparkling crystals and the blue-gray seed beads in this anklet capture this beautiful sight. Peyote stitch, netting, and right-angle weave are all you need to create the bezels for large raindrop-shaped crystals and the stunning array of crystals in between.

TOOLS

Beader's Tool Kit (page 2)

Size 12 beading needles

2 pairs of chain-nose or flat-nose pliers

TECHNIQUES

Tubular peyote stitch (page 7)

Netting (page 8)

Right-angle weave (RAW) (page 10)

INSTRUCTIONS

Make the Large Rain Drop Bezels

1. Needle up a wingspan of thread and pick up 43B. Stitch through the first three beads again to form a loop **(Fig. 1, pink thread)**. Leave a tail thread just long enough to weave into your beadwork later.

SKILL LEVEL

Intermediate

DIMENSIONS

9 inches (22.9 cm) long and 3 inches (6.7 cm) wide

MATERIALS

10 g nickel-plated size 15⁰ seed beads (A)

12 g opaque smoke gray luster size 11⁰ cylinder beads (B)

4 g dyed silver-lined smoky opal size 11⁰ seed beads (C)

3 crystal teardrop fancy stones, crystal foiled, 22 × 11 mm

5 crystal teardrop fancy stones, crystal foiled, 18 × 9 mm

7 crystal teardrop fancy stones, crystal foiled, 14 × 7 mm

7 blue shade crystal drop pendants, 13 × 6.5 mm

6 blue shade crystal drop pendants, 11 × 5.5 mm

2 or more silver-plated jump rings, 8 mm

1 or more silver-plated jump rings, 3 mm

1 silver-plated jewelry hook, 10 mm

Crystal braided fishing line thread, 6 lb

Symbols

○ A
▢ B
◯ C

Fig. 1

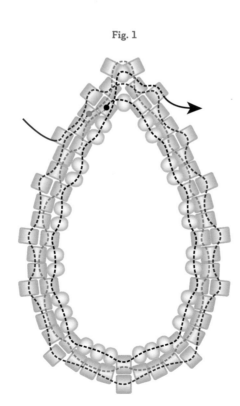

2. Pick up 1B, skip the next B in the loop, and stitch through the B after it. Pick up 2B and stitch through the very next B in the initial loop to form the point of the bezel. Work four peyote stitches, using 1B for each and passing through 2B in the initial loop after adding each bead; four peyote stitches, using 1B for each and passing through 3B in the initial loop after adding each new bead; and four peyote stitches using 1B for each and passing through 2B in the initial loop after adding each bead. Step up through the first B added in this round **(Fig. 1, blue thread)**.

3. Pick up 1A. Stitch through the next single B that was peyote stitched in the previous row. This will bring your thread to the inside of the bezel, where you will continue to work. Work four peyote stitches using 2A for each stitch, four peyote stitches using 3A for each stitch, and four peyote stitches using 2A for each stitch. Do not step up; stitch through the next B. Pick up 1A and stitch through the other B in the pair, so the new A sits on the pair of B added in step 2. Stitch through the next B on the outer edge of the bezel **(Fig. 1, black thread)**.

4. Turn the beadwork over to work on the back side. Work four peyote stitches using 2B for each, four peyote stitches using 3B for each, and five peyote stitches using 2B for each. When adding the fifth pair of 2B, skip the 2B centered at the tip of the bezel and pass through the next single B. Step up through the first pair of B added this round **(Fig. 2, pink thread)**.

5. Work three peyote stitches, using 1B for each and passing through 2B in the previous round after adding each bead; four peyote stitches, using 1B for each and passing through the next 3B in the previous round after adding each bead; and four peyote stitches using 1B for each and passing through the next 2B in the previous round. Pick up 1B and stitch through the first B in the next pair of B in the previous round. Pick up 2B and stitch through the second B in the same pair. Pick up 1B and stitch through the next pair of B. Step up through the first B added in this round **(Fig. 2, black thread)**. Put one 22 × 11–mm crystal teardrop in the bezel, face down, aligning the stone's point with the point of the bezel.

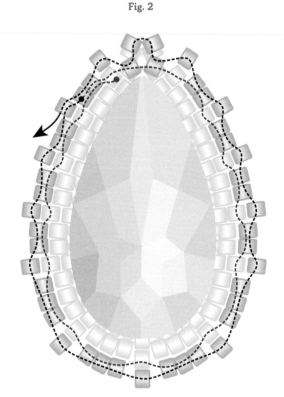

Fig. 2

6. Work three peyote stitches using 2A for each, four peyote stitches using 3A for each, and four peyote stitches using 2A for each. Pick up 1A and stitch through the next B in the previous round; this bead should fall right at the point of the stone. Pick up 2A and stitch through the next B in the previous round. Step up through the first 2A added this round **(Fig. 3, pink thread)**.

7. Work two peyote stitches, using 1A and passing through the next 2A in the previous round after adding each new bead; work four peyote stitches, using 1A for each and passing through the next 3A in the previous round after adding each new bead; and work four peyote stitches using 1A for each stitch and passing through the next 2A in the previous round after adding each new bead. Pick up 1A and stitch through the next A in the previous round. Pick up 1A and stitch through the next 2A in the previous round. Repeat once. Step up through the first A added in the previous round, then stitch through the next 2A in the previous round and next A in this round **(Fig. 3, black thread)**.

8. Pick up 8A. Stitch through the A directly opposite the point of the bezel. Pick up another 8A and stitch through the third single A over, added in the previous round to the side of the bezel. Pick up 10A and stitch through the 2A added at the point of the bezel. Pick up another 10A and stitch through the A at which you started this step. Step up through the first 3A added **(Fig. 4, blue thread)**.

9. Pick up 1C and stitch through the sixth A added in the adjacent group of 8A. Pick up 1C and stitch through the third A in the next group of 10A. Pick up 1C and stitch through the eighth A in the following group of 10A. Pick up 1C and stitch through the third A in the first group of 8A added in the previous step **(Fig. 4, pink thread)**.

10. Stitch through the next 5A in the group of 8A, the next A in the bezel, the next group of 3A in the previous round, the next B in the round before, and the next three B in the following round **(Fig. 4, black thread)**.

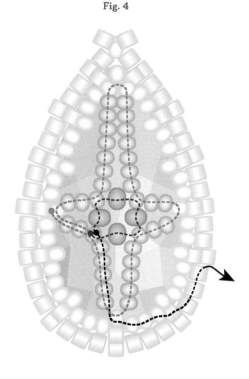

Fig. 3

Fig. 4

11. Peyote stitch 1C in the next five ditches of this round, passing through the next 2B in the same round after adding each bead. When you reach the tip of the bezel, pick up 1C and stitch through the next 2B on the other side of the point. Peyote stitch 1C in the next four ditches, passing through the next 2B in the same round. Peyote stitch 1C in the following four ditches, but now pass through the next 3B in the same round **(Fig. 5)**. Leave the working thread hanging for assembly later. Weave in, secure, and trim the tail thread.

12. Repeat steps 1–11 twice to create a total of three large raindrop bezels.

Make the Medium Rain Drop Bezels

13. Needle up a half wingspan of thread and pick up 33B. Stitch through the first 3B again to form a loop **(Fig. 6, pink thread)**. Leave a tail thread just long enough to weave into your beadwork later.

14. Pick up 1B, skip the next B in the loop, and stitch through the next B. Pick up 2B and stitch through the next B in the loop to form the point of the bezel. Work three peyote stitches, using 1B for each and passing through 2B in the initial loop after adding each bead; three peyote stitches, using 1B and passing through the next 3B in the initial loop; and three peyote stitches, using 1B for each and passing through 2B in the initial loop. Step up through the first B added in this round **(Fig. 6, blue thread)**.

15. Pick up 1A and stitch through the next B that was added on the inside of the bezel in the previous round. Work three peyote stitches using 2A for each, three peyote stitches using 3A for each, and three peyote stitches using 2A for each. Stitch through the next B. Pick up 1A and stitch through the next B from the initial loop and the following B, moving toward the outside of the bezel **(Fig. 6, black thread)**.

16. Turn the beadwork over to the back. Work three peyote stitches using 2B for each stitch, three peyote stitches using 3B for each stitch, and four peyote stitches using 2B for each stitch. Step up through the first pair of B added in this round **(Fig. 7, pink thread)**.

17. Work two peyote stitches, using 1B for each and passing through 2B in the previous round; three peyote stitches, using 1B for each and passing through 3B in the previous round; and three peyote stitches, using 1B for each and passing through 2B in the previous round.

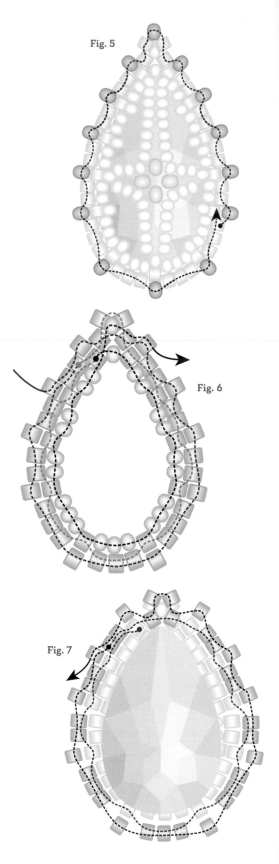

Fig. 5

Fig. 6

Fig. 7

Pick up 1B and stitch through just the first B in the next pair of B added in the previous round. Pick up 2B and stitch through the next B in the same pair in the previous round. Make one peyote stitch with 1B, stitch through the next B, then step up through the first B added in this round **(Fig. 7, black thread)**. Place one 18 × 9–mm crystal teardrop stone in the bezel face down, aligning the points of the stone and bezel.

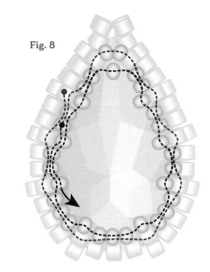

Fig. 8

18. Work two peyote stitches using 2A, three peyote stitches using 3A for each stitch, and three peyote stitches using 2A for each stitch. Pick up 2A and stitch through the next single B in the previous round; the new beads should fall inside the bezel and cover the point of the stone. Peyote stitch one pair of A; step up through the first pair of A added in this round **(Fig. 8, pink thread)**.

19. Work seven peyote stitches using 1A for each stitch and passing through all the beads in each group of 2A or 3A in the previous round. Pick up 1A, skip the next 2A in the previous round, and stitch through the following 2A. Peyote stitch 1A, passing through both beads in the the group of 2A in the previous round. Step up through the first A added in this round, then stitch through the next 2A added in the previous round, and the next A added in this round **(Fig. 8, black thread)**.

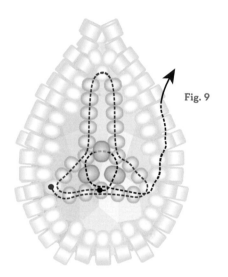

Fig. 9

20. Pick up 5A and stitch through the third A away in the previous round. Pick up 8A and stitch through the third A away added in the previous round. Pick up 8A and stitch through the A at which you started. Step up through the first 3A added **(Fig. 9, pink thread)**.

21. Pick up 1C and stitch through the third A in the adjacent group of 8A. Pick up 1C and stitch through the sixth A in the next group of 8A. Pick up 1C and stitch through the A at which you started. Then stitch through the next 2A in the group of 5A, the next 3A in the bezel, and the next 3B, moving toward the front side of the bezel **(Fig. 9, black thread)**.

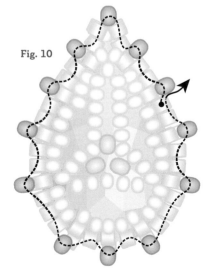

Fig. 10

22. Peyote stitch 1C in the next seven ditches in the same round, including the ditch at the point of the bezel. Peyote stitch 1C in the ditch, but only stitch through one B of the next 3B after adding the new C. Pick up 1C, skip the next B in the group of 3B in the round, and stitch through the third B. Peyote stitch 1C in the next three ditches in the same round. Leave your working thread hanging for assembly. Weave in, secure, and trim your tail thread **(Fig. 10)**.

23. Repeat steps 13–22 four more times to create a total of five medium raindrop bezels.

Make the Small Rain Drop Bezels

24. Needle up a half wingspan of thread and pick up 27B. Stitch through the first 3B again to form a loop **(Fig. 11, pink thread)**. Leave a tail thread just long enough to weave in, secure, and trim later.

25. Peyote stitch 1B. Pick up 2B and stitch through the next B in the initial loop to form the point of the bezel. Work two peyote stitches, using 1B for each and passing through the next 2B in the initial loop after adding the bead; three peyote stitches using 1B for each and passing through the next 3B in the initial loop; and two peyote stitches using 1B for each and passing through the next 2B in the initial loop. Step up through the first B added in this round, moving toward the inside of the bezel **(Fig. 11, blue thread)**.

26. Pick up 1A and stitch through the next single B added in the previous round. Work two peyote stitches using 2A for each, three peyote stitches using 3A for each, and two peyote stitches using 2A for each. Stitch through the next B in the previous round, moving toward the point of the bezel. Pick up 1A and stitch through the next B in the same round, then the following B on the outer edge of the bezel **(Fig. 11, black thread)**.

27. Turn the beadwork over to the back. Work two peyote stitches using 2B for each, three peyote stitches using 3B for each, and three peyote stitches using 2B for each. Step up through the first pair of B added **(Fig. 12, pink thread)**.

Fig. 11

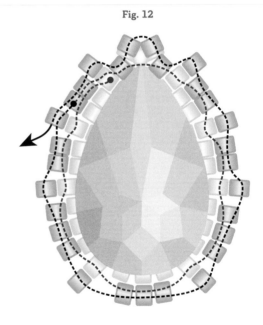

Fig. 12

28. Work one peyote stitch, using 1B and passing through the next 2B in the previous round after adding the new bead; three peyote stitches, using 1B and passing through the next 3B in the previous round after adding the new bead; and two peyote stitches, using 1B and passing through the next 2B in the previous round after adding the new bead. Pick up 1B and stitch through the first B in the next pair of B in the previous round. Pick up 2B and stitch through the next B in the same pair of B in the previous round. Peyote stitch 1B, then step up through the first B added in this round **(Fig. 12, black thread)**. Place one 14 × 7-mm crystal teardrop stone in the bezel face down, aligning the stone's point with the point of the bezel.

29. Work one peyote stitch using 2A, work three peyote stitches using 3A, and two peyote stitches using 2A for each. Stitch directly through the next single B in the previous round. Work one peyote stitch with 2A. Step up through the first 2A added in this round **(Fig. 13, pink thread)**.

30. Pick up 4A and stitch through the middle A in the second group of 3A added in the previous round. Pick up 4A and stitch through the next pair of A in the previous round. Pick up 3A and stitch through the pair of A at which you started this step. Stitch through the next B in the previous round and the next 3B, moving toward the front of the bezel **(Fig. 13, black thread)**.

31. Peyote stitch 1C in the ditch, passing through just the first B in the next group of 3B (outlined in pink in **Fig. 14**) to complete the stitch. Pick up 1C and stitch through the third B in the same group of 3B. Peyote stitch 1C in the eight remaining ditches in the same round, including the ditch at the point of the bezel **(Fig. 14)**. Leave your working thread hanging. Weave in, secure, and trim the tail thread.

32. Repeat steps 24–31 six more times to create a total of seven small raindrop bezels.

Assembly

33. Arrange the three large bezels (lg.), five medium bezels (md.), and seven small bezels (sm.) as shown in **Figure 15**. You will use the hanging working threads to secure the bezels with RAW units and swags made from seed beads and drop pendants.

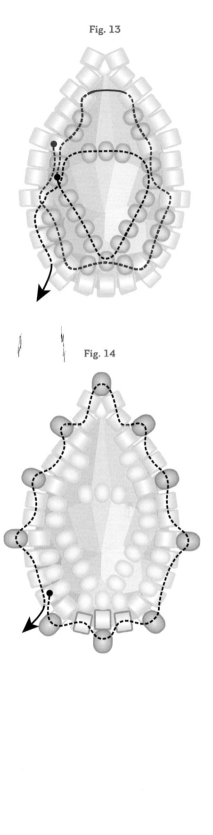

Fig. 13

Fig. 14

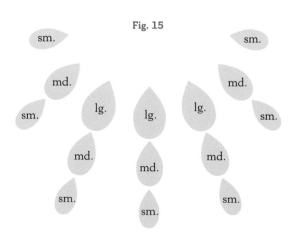

Fig. 15

sm. sm.

md. md.

sm. lg. lg. lg. sm.

md. md.

sm. md. sm.

sm.

First Row of Bezels

34. You will first connect the three large bezels in the first row together. Bring your working thread out of the second C from the point on a large bezel. Pick up 3C. Stitch through the C on the bezel again in a circular fashion to form a RAW unit, then pass through the first 2C added. Create three more RAW units with C. To form the fifth RAW unit, pick up 1C and stitch through the second C from the point on the next large bezel, then pick up another C and stitch through the C in the last RAW unit. Stitch through the next C and the C on the bezel again **(Fig. 16)**.

35. Pick up 1A. Stitch through the C across the RAW unit, moving into the bead on the side opposite from where your thread is emerging, to add the A in the center of the fifth RAW unit. Repeat four times to add an A to the remaining four RAW units **(Fig. 17)**. Leave the thread hanging for adding swags or attaching more bezels later.

36. Repeat steps 34–35 to attach the remaining large bezel.

37. Following the method outlined in steps 34–35, make four RAW units to connect one medium bezel to each side of the joined large bezels. Connect one small bezel to each of the medium bezels using the same method and four RAW units as well.

38. Create a chain of ten RAW units on the opposite side of one of the small bezels, starting with the second C from the point of the bezel. Create a chain of six RAW units on the opposite side of the other small bezel. Leave the threads hanging to attach the clasp later.

Tip: If you need to lengthen your anklet, you can add a few additional RAW units to each side of the chain.

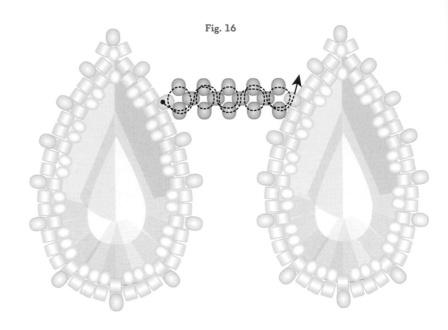

Fig. 16

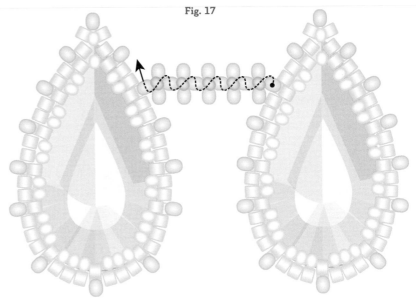

Fig. 17

Second and Third Rows of Bezels

39. You will join one medium bezel to the bottom of each large bezel. Weave the working thread on the large bezel to the center C at the bottom of the bezel. Pick up 1C and stitch through the C at the tip of the medium bezel. Pick up 1C and stitch through the C at the bottom of the large bezel again to form a RAW unit. Pick up 1A. Stitch through the C at the top of the medium bezel, moving into the bead from the side opposite of where your thread is emerging, to add it to the center of the RAW unit **(Fig. 18, blue thread)**. Repeat to join the remaining medium bezels.

40. You will now join a small bezel to the bottom of the two medium bezels in the first row and the three medium bezels in the second row. Weave through the outside of the medium bezel to the center C at the bottom of the bezel **(Fig. 18, pink thread)**. Repeat step 39, using the C at the top of the small bezel and the center C at the bottom of the medium bezel to create a RAW unit that joins the two bezels **(Fig. 18, black thread)**. Repeat to join the remaining small bezels. Leave the working thread in case you can use it for adding the swags.

Add the Swags

41. Pick up the hanging thread on or near a large bezel and weave it to the second C away from the RAW units on the large bezel's edge, moving away from the point of the bezel **(Fig. 19, pink thread)**.

42. Pick up four repeats of [1A, 1B], 1A, one 13 × 6.5–mm drop pendant, 1A, and four repeats of [1B, 1A]. Stitch through the second C below the RAW strip connecting the two large bezels, toward the point of the bezel **(Fig. 19, blue thread)**. Pick up 1A and stitch back through the last C, all the beads just added, and the C on the first bezel. Pick up 1A and stitch back through the same C **(Fig. 19, black thread)**. Leave the thread hanging in case you need to add another swag; otherwise, weave into the bezel, secure, and trim. Repeat this step to add a swag between the two remaining large bezels.

Fig. 18

Fig. 19

43. Repeat steps 41–42 to add a swag between each outside large bezel and adjacent medium bezel in the first row, but use three repeats of [1A, 1B] and [1B, 1A] instead of four.

44. Repeat steps 41–42 to add a swag between each medium bezel and adjacent small bezel in the first row, but use the smaller 11 × 5.5–mm drop pendant and three repeats of [1A, 1B] and [1B, 1A] instead of four. When attaching the swag to the small bezel, stitch through the C directly below the RAW units connecting the small bezel to the medium bezel instead of the second C below the connection point.

45. To add a swag between a small bezel at the end of the anklet and the RAW chain at that end, pick up the working thread on the small bezel and bring it out of the C below the C to which the RAW chain is attached, heading away from the point of the bezel. Pick up three repeats of: [1A, 1B], 1A, one 11 × 5.5–mm drop pendant, 1A, and three repeats of [1B, 1A]. Stitch through the C between the fifth and sixth units in the RAW chain and the next 3C in the sixth RAW unit, then back through all the new beads added and the C on the small bezel. Pick up 1A and stitch back through the C on the small bezel. Retrace the thread path once more to reinforce, then weave in, secure, and trim the thread. Repeat this step to add a swag to the other end of the anklet.

46. For the second row of bezels, repeat steps 41–42 using five repeats of [1A, 1B] and [1B, 1A] instead of four to add a swag between the third C from the tip of the center medium bezel and the corresponding C in each of the other two medium bezels. Do the same, but use the 11 × 5.5–mm drop pendent, to add a swag between the third C from the tip of the medium bezels and the second C away from the tip of the small bezels on each side of the row.

Attach the Clasp

47. Needle up the working thread on the chain of six RAW units at one end of the anklet. Pick up 5A and the loop of the jewelry hook, then stitch through the end C on the last RAW unit. Stitch through the loop of 5A at least twice more, then weave in, secure, and trim the thread.

48. Needle up the working thread on the chain of ten RAW units on the other end of the anklet. Pick up 5A and one of the 8-mm jump rings. Stitch through the end C in the last RAW unit. Stitch through the loop of 5A at least twice more, then weave in, secure, and trim the thread.

49. With the pliers, open one 3-mm jump ring and close it around the 8-mm jump ring on the end of the anklet. Open another 8-mm jump ring, string one 11 × 5.5–mm drop pendant and the 3-mm jump ring attached to the anklet. Close the 8-mm jump ring. If you need a longer anklet, alternate between adding 3-mm and 8-mm jump rings in a chain until the anklet is the desired length. Remember to move the 11 × 5.5–mm drop pendant to the last 8-mm jump ring added.

Tip: To wear the design as a necklace, make two lengths of chain using jump rings and attach one length to each end of the anklet before you add the clasp.

Bracelets

Ocean Waves Bracelet

I am instinctually drawn to the ocean and captivated by its vastness, danger, and beauty. The sound of the ocean waves lapping up on a beach is soothing, and the feeling of floating in the water incredibly comforting and relaxing. This bracelet captures the imagery of waves crashing onto a sandy beach.

TECHNIQUES

Netting (page 8)

Peyote stitch (page 5)

Three-sided prismatic right-angle weave (PRAW-3) (page 12)

INSTRUCTIONS

Make the Wave Pieces

1. Needle up a wingspan and a half of braided fishing line thread and pick up 3A. Stitch through the first A again to form a loop, leaving about 18 inches (46 cm) of tail thread. This is the base of your first PRAW-3 unit.

2. Pick up 1B and 2A and stitch through the A in the base again **(Fig. 1)**. This is the first wall.

3. Stitch through the next A in the base **(Fig. 2)**.

4. Pick up 2A and stitch back through the B toward the base, then through the next A in the base **(Fig. 3)**. This is the second wall.

Symbols

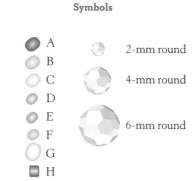

- A
- B
- C
- D
- E
- F
- G
- H

- 2-mm round
- 4-mm round
- 6-mm round

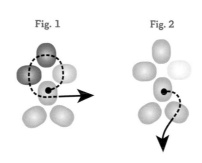

Fig. 1   Fig. 2

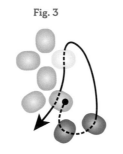

Fig. 3

SKILL LEVEL

Intermediate

DIMENSIONS

6 1/2 inches (16.5 cm) long and 1/2 inch (1.3 cm) wide

MATERIALS

4 g turquoise-lined crystal size 11o seed beads (A)

1 g silver-lined aqua opal size 11o seed beads (B)

1 g ceylon aqua size 11o seed beads (C)

1 g mint-lined crystal size 15o seed beads (D)

2 g luminous ocean blue size 15o seed beads (E)

2 g silver-lined crystal size 15o seed beads (F)

2 g gilt-lined opal size 8o seed beads (G)

2 g bronze size 11o cylinder beads (H)

10 metallic light gold 2X crystal rounds, 2 mm

10 metallic light gold 2X crystal rounds, 4 mm

5 metallic light gold 2X crystal rounds, 6 mm

1 Czech dome bead or other glass cabochon of your choice, 12 mm

Crystal braided fishing line thread, 6 lb

TOOLS

Beader's Tool Kit (page 2)

Size 12 beading needles

5. Stitch through the next A in the base, then up through the second A added in step 2 **(Fig. 4)**.

6. Pick up 1A and stitch back through the first A added in step 4, the A in the base, and the second A added in step 2 **(Fig. 5)**. This is the third wall.

7. Pull the threads tightly to firm up the unit. It should have three sides with four beads in each, a triangular base of three beads, and a triangular top of three beads. The top becomes the base for the next unit. Step up through the next A in the top to get ready for the next unit **(Fig. 6)**.

8. Create a PRAW-3 rope with a total of 57 units, using 3A for the base and the following sequence of beads for the sides of each unit: [1B, 1A, 1A] for the first side, [1A, 1A] for the second side, and 1A for the third side. Leave an 18-inch (46 cm) tail at the start. All the B on the rope should line up and form the "spine" of the tube. This will create a 6½-inch (16.5 cm) bracelet. For a longer bracelet, add additional units in multiples of 11; each group of 11 units adds approximately an inch (2.5 cm) to the bracelet. After adding the last unit, stitch down the A opposite from the last B **(Fig. 7)**.

9. Pick up 2H. Stitch through the next A along the length of the tube, filling in the gap between the A with the 2H. Repeat once. Make a peyote stitch with 1H in each of the next nine spaces, pulling tightly as you go. The units with 2H should curve one way and the units with single H should curve in the opposite direction. After adding the last H, stitch around through the four beads that form one side of the PRAW unit, pulling tightly to secure the curves created **(Fig. 8)**. Repeat from the beginning of the step four more times (or until you reach the second to last space if you added more than 57 units to your PRAW-3 rope). Pick up 2H. Stitch through the next A.

10. Repeat once, filling in the gap between the A. Stitch through the next 2A on the wall of the last PRAW-3 unit **(Fig. 9)**.

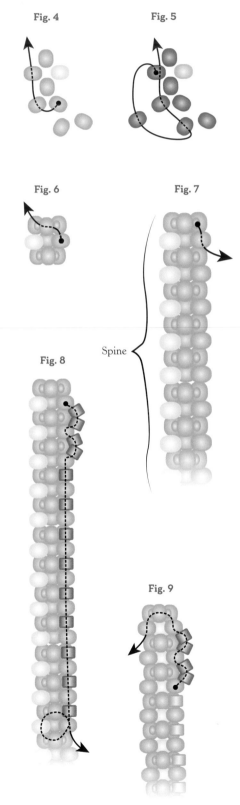

Fig. 4

Fig. 5

Fig. 6

Fig. 7

Fig. 8

Spine

Fig. 9

11. Repeat step 9 to work the other side of the rope. Then turn around at the end and stitch through the first 3B without adding any beads **(Fig. 10)**.

12. Pick up one D and stitch through the next B. Pick up 3D and stitch through the next B; add six more groups of 3D in this manner. Then pick up 1D and stitch through the next 3B **(Fig. 11)**. Repeat from the beginning of the step until you reach the end of the bracelet.

13. Stitch around the four beads in the wall of the last unit to reverse direction. Stitch back through the second-to-last B and third-to-last B, then the next D **(Fig. 12, red thread)**. Pick up 1E and 1C and stitch through the middle D in the group of 3D added in the previous step. Pick up 1E, 1C, and 1E and stitch through the middle D in the group of 3D added in the previous step; add five more groups of [1E, 1C, 1E] in this manner. Then pick up 1C and 1E and stitch through the single D added in step 12 **(Fig. 12, black thread)**.

14. Pick up 1E, 1C, and 1E, skip over the next 3B, and then stitch through the next single D added in step 12 **(Fig. 13)**.

15. Repeat steps 13 and 14 until you reach the end of the bracelet. After passing through the last single D, reverse direction by stitching through the next B, the four beads that form the wall of the second to last PRAW-3 unit, and back through the B again. Stitch back through the single D from which you started, then the last E and C added **(Fig. 14)**.

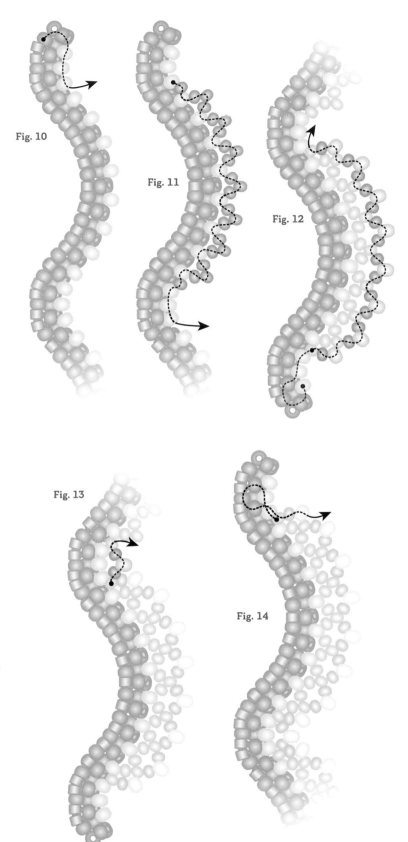

Fig. 10

Fig. 11

Fig. 12

Fig. 13

Fig. 14

16. Pick up 1E, 1G, and 1E; stitch through the next C. Repeat six times **(Fig. 15, black thread)**.

17. Pick up 1C and 1E. Stitch through the next C. Pick up 1E and 1C and stitch through the next C **(Fig. 15, red thread)**.

18. Repeat steps 16 and 17 along the entire length of the bracelet, ending with an iteration of step 16. Stitch through the next E, D, and B. Reverse direction by stitching around the wall of the second to last PRAW-3 unit, then head back through the next B, D, E, C, E, and G **(Fig. 16)**.

19. Pick up 3F and stitch through the next G. Repeat five times. Pick up 3F and stitch through the next C **(Fig. 17, black thread)**. Pick up 2F and stitch through the next C. Pick up 3F and stitch through the next G **(Fig. 17, red thread)**. Repeat this step until you reach the end of the bracelet, ending after you add a group of 3F.

20. Repeat steps 1–19 to make a second wave piece.

Join the Two Wave Pieces

21. Needle up a new wingspan of thread, weaving it into the beadwork and securing it near the end of a wave component that is opposite from the one with the hanging tail thread. (You can also use the hanging working thread if you have at least a yard [91.4 cm].) Heading in the direction toward the end of the PRAW-3 rope, bring the thread out of the last 2H on the end of the piece.

22. Line up the other wave piece next to the first; the two pairs of H on one component should be sitting right next to the two pairs of H on the other. Heading toward the opposite end of the bracelet, stitch through the adjacent pair of H on the second wave piece. Pick up one H and stitch through the next pair of H on the same wave piece **(Fig. 18, black thread)**. Reverse

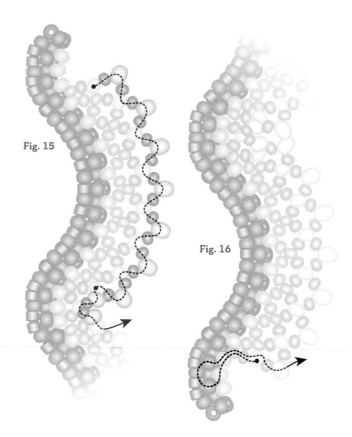

Fig. 15

Fig. 16

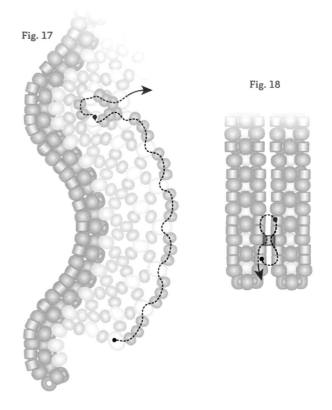

Fig. 17

Fig. 18

direction and stitch through the adjacent pair of H on the first wave piece. Stitch through the newly added H and the next pair of H on the same wave piece so that you've completed a circle **(Fig. 18, red thread)**. Retrace the thread path at least twice to reinforce.

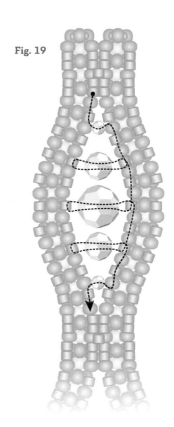

Fig. 19

23. Weave through the PRAW-3 rope to each pair of H and repeat step 22 to continue joining the wave pieces. After joining the last pairs, weave through the beadwork to the first H inside the openings between the joined sections of the wave pieces, working in the direction toward the opposite end of the bracelet. Pick up one 2-mm crystal round and stitch across through the next A on the second wave piece. Pass through the next H, A, and H. Pick up one 4-mm crystal round and stitch through the corresponding H across on the second wave piece, then back through the 4-mm crystal round and H on the first wave piece. Stitch through the next A, H, A, and H. Pick up one 6-mm crystal round and stitch through the corresponding H across on the second wave piece, then back through the 6-mm crystal round and the H on the first wave piece. Stitch through the next A, H, A, and H. Add another 4-mm crystal round as described earlier, then stitch through the next A, H, and A. Pick up one 2-mm crystal round and stitch through the next H across on the second wave piece **(Fig. 19)**. Repeat the thread path through the crystal rounds and their adjoining beads for security.

24. Repeat step 23 in each opening between the joined sections. Leave the working thread hanging to attach the toggle button later.

Make the Toggle

25. Make the toggle loop. Weave through one wave piece until you reach the end of the PRAW-3 rope that is opposite from the end with the tail thread from step 1. Add 14 PRAW-3 units as described in step 1. Join the last unit to the end unit on the other wave piece. Pick up 1A and stitch through the next A on the last PRAW-3 unit on the wave piece. Pick up another A and stitch through the A on the end of the toggle loop. Then stitch through the first A added and the next A in the end unit of the set of waves **(Fig. 20)**.

Fig. 20

26. Pick up 1B and stitch through the A below on the newly added PRAW-3 unit. Stitch through the first A added in the previous step and the A with which you started to form a circular thread path. Stitch through the next A. Make sure the B is lined up with the other B in the toggle loop **(Fig. 21)**.

27. Turn the beadwork over and stitch through the B and the 3A that form the third side of the unit you just formed **(Fig. 22)**. Weave in, secure, and trim your thread.

28. To make the toggle button, needle up a half wingspan of thread and pick up 30H. Stitch through the first 2H or 3H again to form a loop to begin creating the bezel, leaving just enough of a tail thread to weave into the beadwork; secure the tail thread **(Fig. 23, black thread)**. Make one round of peyote stitch along the inside of the loop, using 1F for each stitch; this round will be in the front of the dome bead. Do not step up. Instead stitch through the next H so your thread is on the outside of the loop **(Fig. 23, blue thread)**.

29. Working toward the back side of the bezel, peyote stitch one round of A; step up through the first A added **(Fig. 23, pink thread)**. Peyote stitch a second round of A; step up through the first A added in the second round **(Fig. 23, brown thread)**. Peyote stitch one round of H, pulling tightly to start shaping the bezel **(Fig. 23, red thread)**. Put your dome bead into the beadwork, dome side down, then peyote stitch a round of F, pulling very tightly to close the back of the bezel around the dome bead; step up through the first F added in the round **(Fig. 23, green thread)**.

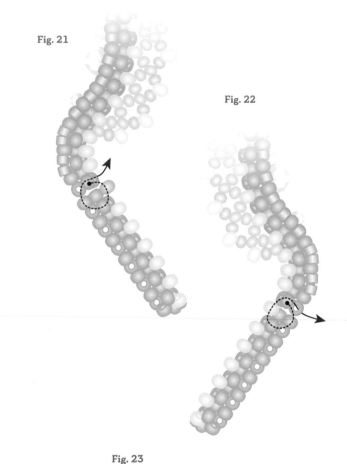

Fig. 21

Fig. 22

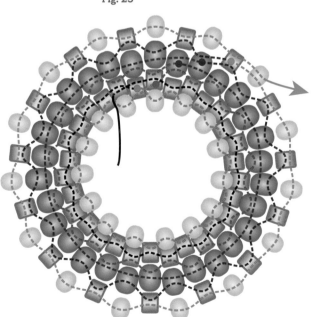

Fig. 23

30. To create the back of the bezel, pick up 9F, skip the next four F in the previous round, and stitch through the fifth F. Repeat twice, then step up through the first 5F added **(Fig. 24, red thread)**. Stitch through the middle F in the next group of 9F, then the middle F in the last group of 9F. Stitch through the middle F in the first group of 9F again **(Fig. 24, black thread)**. Retrace the thread path at least twice to reinforce, then weave in, secure, and trim your thread.

31. Needle up the tail thread that you left hanging in step 1; this should be the end of the bracelet opposite from the one with the toggle loop. Bring the thread out of the A above the last pair of H connecting the wave pieces. Pick up 6A and stitch through the 3F in the center of the back of the toggle button. Then stitch back through the last A. Pick up 5A and stitch through the A above the last pair of H on the other wave piece and the next 2H. Reverse direction and stitch through the adjacent pair of H and the next A on the first wave piece **(Fig. 25)**. Retrace the thread path at least twice to reinforce. Weave in, secure, and trim all hanging threads.

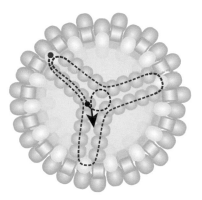

Fig. 24

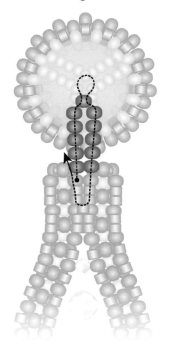

Fig. 25

Vine Wrap Bracelet

In wild areas of the world with abundant rainfall, you can almost always find a leafy vine winding along the ground, creeping up neighboring bushes, or growing in thick, curling ropes that hang from trees. There are few things as beautiful to behold as a verdant forest adorned with these plants. Their spiraling patterns and leafy growth inspired this wrap bracelet. It uses seed beads to capture the fractal patterns created by twisting and overlapping spirals, achieving an incredibly lush yet wearable look.

INSTRUCTIONS

Make the Main Vine

1. The Main Vine is stitched with a two-ladder tubular herringbone stitch with a twisted pattern. Needle up a wingspan of thread and pick up 3A, 1B, 3A, and 2B. Stitch through the first 3A again to form a loop. Leave about 12 inches (30.5 cm) of thread for attaching the clasp later **(Fig. 1)**. The first four beads will become Ladder 1 of your herringbone rope. The fifth through ninth beads will become Ladder 2 of your rope **(Fig. 2)**.

2. Pick up 1A and 1B. Stitch through the next B and 3A of the initial loop **(Fig. 3, pink thread)**. Pick up another 1A and 1B and stitch through the next B in the initial loop. Skip the next B and next A and stitch through the next 2A (which are the second and third bead of the initial loop). Step up through the first A added in this round **(Fig. 3, black thread)**.

Symbols

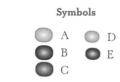

A   D
B   E
C

Fig. 1

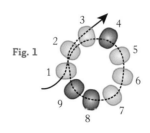

Fig. 2

Ladder 1

Ladder 2

Fig. 3

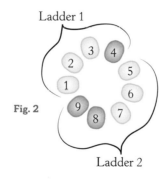

Ladder 1

Skip

Ladder 2

SKILL LEVEL

Intermediate

DIMENSIONS

1¾ inches (4.4 cm) wide and 23 inches (58.4 cm) long

MATERIALS

7 g higher metallic carnival size 11º seed beads (A)

6 g bronze antique gold size 11º seed beads (B)

9 g higher metallic matte Mardi Gras size 11º seed beads (C)

5 g higher metallic carnival size 15º seed beads (D)

7 g metallic dark raspberry size 15º seed beads (E)

1 magnetic ball clasp or push pull clasp

Smoke braided fishing line thread, 6 lb

TOOLS

Beader's Tool Kit (page 2)

Size 12 beading needles

TECHNIQUES

Netting (page 8)

Right-angle weave (RAW) (page 10)

Tubular herringbone stitch (page 9)

3. Pinch your beadwork together so that the two pairs of beads you added in the previous step come closer together. They will form the top of your two ladders. Continue herringbone stitch by picking up 1A and 1B, then stitching down through the next B. Stitch up through the top 3A in the next ladder **(Fig. 4)**. Pick up 1A and 1B, then stitch down through the next B. Stitch up through the top 3A in the next ladder.

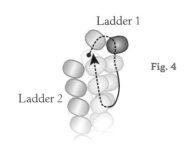

Ladder 1

Ladder 2

Fig. 4

4. Continue this twisted tubular herringbone stitch for three more rows.

5. Pick up 1A and 1B and stitch down through the next B in Ladder 1. Pick up one E and stitch through the third A from the top of the Ladder 2 and the next 2A. This will position the E between the two ladders **(Fig. 5)**.

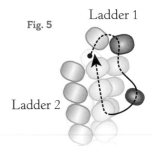

Fig. 5

Ladder 1

Ladder 2

6. Complete one regular herringbone stitch by picking up 1A and 1B, stitching down through the next B in Ladder 2 and up through the top 3A in Ladder 1 **(Fig. 6)**.

7. Pick up 1A and 1B and stitch down through the next B in Ladder 1. Pick up 1C and stitch through the third A from the top of Ladder 2 and the next 2A. This will position the C between ladders **(Fig. 7)**.

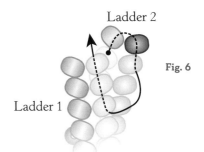

Ladder 2

Ladder 1

Fig. 6

8. Repeat step 3 five times to add ten herringbone stitches, adding 1A and 1B for each stitch. To make it easy to keep track of the beads that you're adding, you can count out the 10A and 10B ahead of time.

9. Repeat steps 5–8 until you can wrap your bracelet loosely around your wrist three times. The bracelet will tighten slightly as you continue your beadwork, so make sure it is loose at this stage.

Make the Large Wrapped Vine

10. When the bracelet is the desired length, weave back to the last C added between the two ladders. Pick up 9C. Working in the direction opposite from how your Main Vine spirals, stitch through the next C on the Main Vine **(Fig. 8)**.

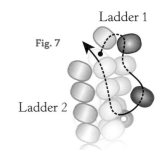

Ladder 1

Fig. 7

Ladder 2

11. Continue adding groups of 9C between each C, working all the way down the length of the Main Vine and pulling tightly as you go to take up any slack.

Fig. 8

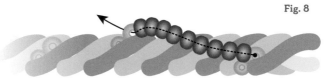

Make the Small Wrapped Vine

12. After stitching through the last C on the Main Vine, reverse direction and stitch through the adjacent E between the two ladders **(Fig. 9, blue thread)**.

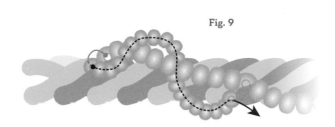

Fig. 9

13. Pick up 18E. Pass your needle over, then under the large wrapped vine. Stitch through the next E between the ladders of the Main Vine. Pull tightly, making sure the thread doesn't catch between the C in the Large Wrapped Vine. If needed, coax the Small Wrapped Vine into place with your finger before proceeding **(Fig. 9, black thread)**.

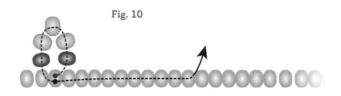

Fig. 10

14. Repeat step 13 until you reach the very last E between the ladders of the Main Vine. Then weave through the beadwork in the Main Vine to turn around and exit through the third or fourth E in the Small Wrapped Vine.

Note: In the subsequent figures, the Small Wrapped Vine is shown as a straight length of strung beads. The beadwork behind it has been omitted for clarity.

15. Pick up 1E, 3D, and 1E. Stitch through the E at which you started this step to form a loop **(Fig. 10, pink thread)**, then stitch through the next 10E as well **(Fig. 10, black thread)**.

16. Repeat step 15 along the length of the Small Wrapped Vine until you reach the other end of the bracelet.

Make the Leaves

17. Start a new thread or weave your working thread into the fourth or fifth C in the Large Wrapped Vine. Stitch three RAW units with 3C in each unit **(Fig. 11, pink thread)**, then one RAW unit with 3D **(Fig. 11, black thread)**. Stitch through the first and third D in the unit to make the middle D stick up.

Note: In the figures, the Large Wrapped Vine is drawn straight and without the beadwork behind it for clarity.

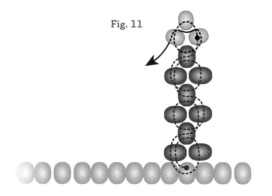

Fig. 11

18. To create the sides of the leaf, pick up 10D and stitch through the first C in the first RAW unit, the C in the Large Wrapped Vine, and the third C in the first RAW unit. Pick up 10D and stitch through the 3D in the last RAW unit **(Fig. 12, blue thread)**. Stitch through the first 3D added in this step **(Fig. 12, black thread)**.

19. To create the veins of the leaf, proceed as follows: Pick up 4D. Stitch through the third C in the second RAW unit, the C at the bottom of the second RAW unit, and the first C in the second RAW unit. Pick up 4D, skip the first 3D in the second group of 10D added in the last step, and stitch through the remaining 7D toward the vine and the third C in the first RAW unit **(Fig. 13, pink thread)**. Stitch through 12C in the vine toward the opposite end of the bracelet **(Fig. 13, black thread)**.

20. Follow the method outlined in steps 17–19 to create Leaf 2, Leaf 3, and Leaf 4. All four leaves are constructed in the same way, but vary in the number of RAW units added, the number of beads on the sides of the leaf, and the number of leaf veins as well as the bead count within each vein.

- **LEAF 2:** Create four RAW units with C and one with D to create the center of the leaf. Add 13D on each side of the leaf. Add the leaf veins using Figure 14 as a reference for the thread path. Each leaf vein has 3D. The first pair of leaf veins start at the third D down from the top of each group of 13D. The second pair of veins start at the third D away from the first pair of veins. Stitch 12C down the Large Wrapped Vine to add the next leaf **(Fig. 14)**.

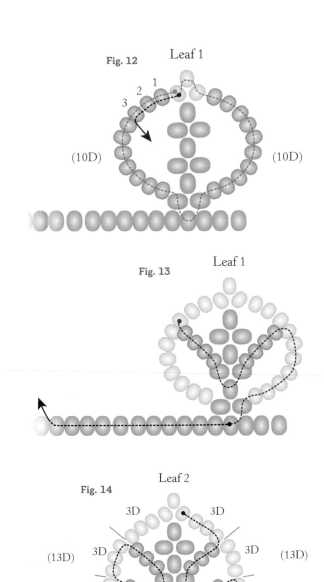

Fig. 12   Leaf 1

(10D)   (10D)

Fig. 13   Leaf 1

Fig. 14   Leaf 2

3D   3D

(13D)   3D   3D   (13D)

- **LEAF 3:** Create five RAW units with C and one with D for the center of the leaf. Add 16D on each side of the leaf. Add the leaf veins using Figure 15 as a reference for the thread path. The first and second leaf veins have 3D each and start at the third D down from the top of each group of 16D. The third and fourth veins have 4D each and start at the fourth D away from the first two veins. The fifth and sixth veins have 4D each and start at the fourth D away from the third and fourth veins. Stitch 12C down the Large Wrapped Vine to add the next leaf **(Fig. 15)**.

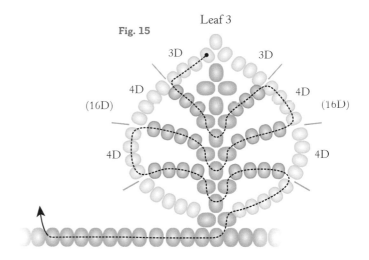

Leaf 3
Fig. 15
3D   3D
4D   4D
(16D)   (16D)
4D   4D

- **LEAF 4:** Create six RAW units with C and one with D. Add 20D on each side of the leaf. Add the leaf veins using Figure 16 as a reference for the thread path. The first and second leaf veins have 4D each and start at the third D down from the top of each group of 20D. The third and fourth veins have 6D each and start at

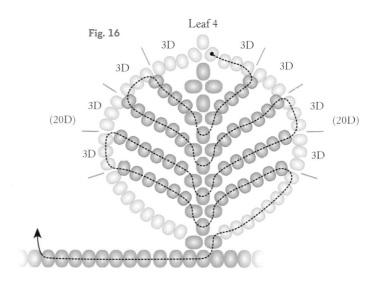

Leaf 4
Fig. 16
3D   3D
3D   3D
3D   3D
(20D)   (20D)
3D   3D

the third D away from the first and second veins. The fifth and sixth veins have 6D each and start at the third D away from the second pair of veins. The seventh and eighth veins have 6D each and start at the third D away from the fifth and sixth veins. Stitch 12C down the Large Wrapped Vine to add the next leaf **(Fig. 16)**.

21. Make four more Leaf 4s, one Leaf 3, one Leaf 2, and one Leaf 1, spacing each leaf 12C apart on the Large Wrapped Vine. Weave the thread into the beadwork of the Main Vine, secure, and trim.

22. To create the remaining leaves for the bracelet, needle up a wingspan of thread and weave it into the opposite end of the bracelet from where you started the first set of leaves. Weave down four or five beads from the start of the Large Wrapped Vine. Make one Leaf 4, one Leaf 3, one Leaf 2, and one Leaf 1, spacing each leaf 12C apart.

23. For the remainder of the vine, create small leaves
to fill the space between the sets of leaves you
created on each end of the bracelet: Pick up 3C
and stitch through the same C in the vine, then
the first C added **(Fig. 17, blue thread)**. Pick
up 1A, 3D, and 1A. Stitch through the third
C in the group of three, then the C in the vine
(Fig. 17, pink thread). Stitch through 11 more
C in the vine **(Fig. 17, black thread)**.

24. Repeat step 23 until you reach the set of leaves
at the opposite end of the bracelet, then weave
in, secure, and trim your thread.

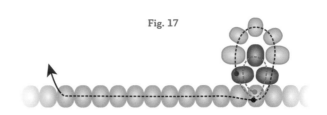

Fig. 17

Add the Clasp

25. Needle up the tail thread and string it through the ring on one side
of the clasp. Stitch through the corresponding B in the other ladder.
Reverse direction and stitch through the adjacent A in the same ladder,
back through the ring on the clasp, and into the B in the first ladder
(Fig. 18). Retrace the thread path at least twice more to reinforce.

26. Stitch up through the third A from the end of the ladder and the next
2A. Pick up 1A and stitch down through the next B **(Fig. 19)**. Repeat
from the beginning of the step, then step up through the first single A
just added.

27. Pick up 3A and stitch through the A in the last row of the opposite
ladder, then the A above this last row **(Fig. 20)**. Repeat to stitch
through the other side of the herringbone tube. Retrace the thread
path around at least once to reinforce, then weave in, secure, and trim
your thread.

28. Start a new 18-inch (45.7 cm) length of thread on the opposite end of
the bracelet. Bring it out of an A in the last row. Repeat steps 25–27 to
attach the other side of the clasp.

Fig. 18   Fig. 19

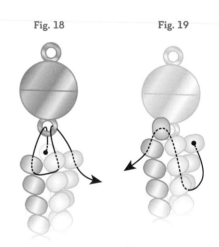

Fig. 20

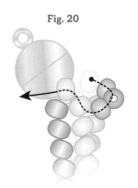

<< *Variation:* To create a simpler bracelet that only wraps around the wrist once, make a shorter version of the Main Vine. Once you have your desired length, follow steps 17–21 and skip to step 24 to add the leaves. Follow the remaining steps to complete the bracelet.

Use the following beads to create this color variation:

A: Sea foam-lined rainbow light topaz size 11° seed beads

B: Semi-glazed rainbow blue turquoise size 11° seed beads

C: Transparent rainbow frosted lime green size 11° seed beads

D: Stable finish silver-lined milky light peridot size 15° seed beads

E: Nickel-plated size 15° seed beads

High Tide Bracelet

There are few creatures as exciting to find in tide pools and beaches as starfish. With their five-fold symmetry and spiky texture, they are a fascinating example of beautiful sea life. This bracelet uses eight starfish-shaped components with sparkling crystal flatbacks that resemble the clear water of the Caribbean, where these amazing creatures can be easily found. Try arranging the starfish in different patterns or changing the placement of the ones with crystals for different looks!

INSTRUCTIONS

Make the Starfish Components

Starfish 1 Component

1. The bracelet is made up of eight separate starfish components. You will construct each component using herringbone stitch to form the arms and netting to form the center. Needle up a half wingspan of thread and pick up five repeats of (1C, 1A). Stitch through the first C again to form a loop **(Fig. 1, pink thread)**. Repeat the thread path to reinforce the loop.

2. Pick up 2A and stitch through the next C. Repeat four times, then step up by stitching through the first A added in this round **(Fig. 1, black thread)**.

Symbols

- A
- B
- C
- D

Fig. 1

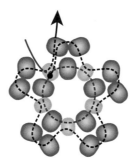

SKILL LEVEL

Intermediate

DIMENSIONS

6 inches (15.2 cm) long and 1¹/₂ inches (3.8 cm) wide

MATERIALS

5 g matte light bronze size 11o seed beads (A)

2 g crystal gold-lined AB size 11o seed beads (B)

1 g crystal gold-lined AB size 15o seed beads (C)

1 g stable finish galvanized eggplant size 15o seed beads (D)

5 blue zircon shimmer round flat back crystals, SS40

Gray nylon beading thread or braided fishing line thread, 4 lb.

TOOLS

Beader's Tool Kit (page 2)

Size 12 beading needles

TECHNIQUES

Tubular herringbone stitch (page 9)

Netting (page 8)

3. Pick up 2A and stitch down through the next A in the previous round. Stitch up through the first A of the next pair of A in the previous round. Repeat four times, then step up through the first A in the previous round and the first A added in this round **(Fig. 2, blue thread)**. This round sets up the five herringbone ladders that become the starfish's arms.

4. Pick up 2A and stitch down through the next A in the previous round. Pick up 1C and stitch up through the first A in the next pair. Repeat four times, then step up through the first A in the previous round and the first A added in the round **(Fig. 2, pink thread)**. Pull tightly. The starfish should start to pucker into a more three-dimensional shape.

5. Repeat step 4 to add the next round, but pick up 2C instead of 1C after you stitch down through the next A in the previous round **(Fig. 2, black thread)**. Pull tightly to continue shaping the starfish. The center will begin to form a dome.

6. Using the herringbone stitch, begin to build the starfish's arms. Pick up 2A. Stitch down through the next A in the previous round and then up through the first A in the previous round and the first A in the pair just added. Pick up 2A and stitch down into the second A added in this round, then stitch through the next 2A. Stitch through the 2C between the arms and up through the top two A in the next ladder. To build the remaining arms, repeat this step four times, then step up through the first A in the first two pairs of A added **(Fig. 3)**. Leave the working thread hanging to assemble the bracelet later.

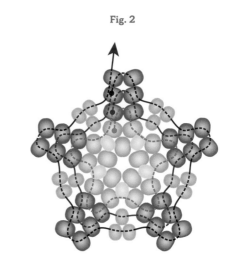

Fig. 2

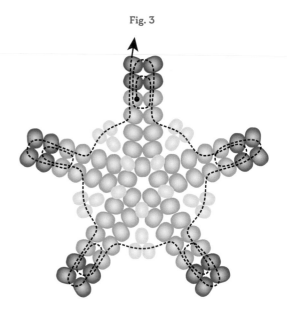

Fig. 3

Starfish 2 Components

7. To make the center of the starfish and begin building the arms, follow steps 1–5.

8. To lengthen the arms, follow step 6, but instead of adding two pairs of A to the each arm, only add one pair of A. This makes the arms of the starfish slightly shorter.

9. Repeat steps 7 and 8 for a total of two Starfish 2 Components.

Starfish 3 Components

10. To make the center of starfish and begin building the arms, follow steps 1–5.

11. Repeat step 10 for a total of two Starfish 3 Components.

Starfish 4 Components

12. To make the center of starfish and begin building the arms, follow steps 1–5.

13. Repeat step 12 twice for a total of three Starfish 4 Components.

Starfish 5 Components

14. Needle up a half wingspan of thread and pick up 10B. Stitch through the first B again to form a loop **(Fig. 4, pink thread)**. Repeat the thread path to reinforce the loop.

15. Pick up 2B, skip the next B, and stitch through the one after it. Repeat four times, then step up through the first B in the first pair added **(Fig. 4, black thread)**.

16. Pick up 2B and stitch down through the next B in the previous round. Pick up 1D and stitch up through the first B in the next pair. Repeat four times, then step up through the first B added in this round **(Fig. 5, blue thread)**.

17. To create an arm, pick up 2B. Stitch down through the next B in the previous round, then stitch up through the first B added in the previous round and the first B added in this round. Repeat from the beginning of this step four times. Pick up 2C and stitch down through the second B of the pair that you just added. Stitch through the next 5B, then the D between arms. Stitch through the first two B in the next arm **(Fig. 5, black thread)**. To build the remaining arms, repeat this step four times.

18. Repeat steps 14–17 for a total of two Starfish 5 Components.

Starfish 6 Component

19. To make the center of the starfish, follow steps 14–16.

20. To create the arms, follow step 17, but do not add the last pair of B and the pair of C in each arm. The arms of this starfish will be shorter.

Starfish 7 Component

21. Needle up a half wingspan of thread and pick up 10A. Stitch through the first A again to form a loop. Repeat the thread path to reinforce the loop.

22. Pick up 2A, skip the next A, and stitch through the following A. Repeat four times, then step up through the first A added in this round.

Fig. 4

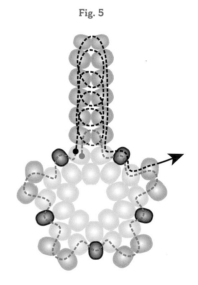

Fig. 5

23. You will now begin to build the arms of the starfish. Pick up 2A and stitch down through the next A in the previous round. Pick up 1C and stitch up through the first A in the next pair. Repeat four times, then step up through the first A added in this round **(Fig. 6, pink thread)**.

24. Pick up 2A and stitch down through the next A in the previous round. Pick up 1A, 1B, and 1A and stitch up through the first A in the top pair in the next arm. Repeat four times, then step up through the first A added in this round **(Fig. 6, black thread)**.

25. Pick up 2A and stitch down through the next A in the previous round. Pick up 4C and stitch up through the first A on the top of the next arm. The 4C should fall on top of the group of A, B, and A in the previous round, between the arms of the starfish. Repeat four times, checking the placement of each group of 4C. Step up through the first A added in this round **(Fig. 7, pink thread)**.

26. Pick up 2A and stitch down through the next A in the previous round. Stitch up through the first bead in the same pair, then through the first A just added. Pick up 2A and stitch down through the next 3A. Stitch through the 4C between the arms, then through the top 2A in the next arm **(Fig. 7, black thread)**. Repeat four times.

27. Turn the beadwork over so the groups of A, B, and A between the arms are on the front side. Weave through the beads to exit the B at the center of one of those groups. *Pick up 1D, 1A, and 1D. Stitch through the A in the next group of three beads. Repeat from * four times. Place one flat back crystal faceup on the center of the starfish **(Fig. 8)**. Pull the thread tightly to bring the added beads together so they hold the edges of the crystal down. Stitch around through the round again at least once to reinforce, pulling tightly to bring the beads as close together as possible.

28. Stitch through the next A, then through the A in the nearest arm. Exit from the tip of the arm **(Fig. 9)**.

Starfish 8 Components

29. To make the center of the starfish, follow steps 21–25.

30. Pick up 2A and stitch down through the next 3A. Stitch through the 4C between the arms of the starfish, then the top 2A in the next arm. Repeat from the beginning of this step four times.

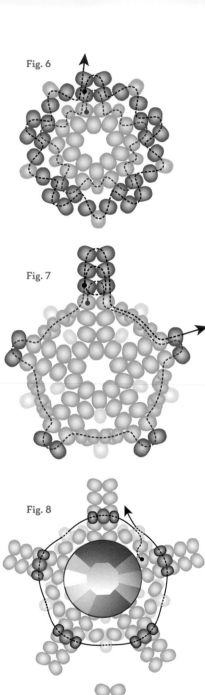

Fig. 6

Fig. 7

Fig. 8

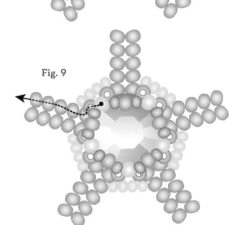

Fig. 9

31. Follow steps 27–28 to finish the component. Leave the working thread hanging to assemble the bracelet later.

32. Repeat steps 29–31 for a total of two Starfish 8 Components.

Assembly

33. The starfish components are connected at the tip of each starfish arm. Review **Fig. 10**, which shows the overall construction of the bracelet. The arrangement of the starfish helps create the random, natural look of this bracelet.

34. Set one Starfish 8 Component aside to use as the clasp button. Referring to **Fig. 10**, you will attach all the other starfish together by following the instructions listed on pages 84–85 for each starfish component, starting at the end of the bracelet with the Starfish 1 component.

When you attach the neighboring components, you will only add new A beads to the arms that are not joined with the arms of other starfish. For arms that will be attached to other starfish components, you will stitch through the A that is already in place on the neighboring starfish; in other words, arms that serve as attachment points will share an A with its neighboring component. **Fig. 11** shows an example of a thread path used to add A beads to a Starfish 2 component and attach it to its neighbor.

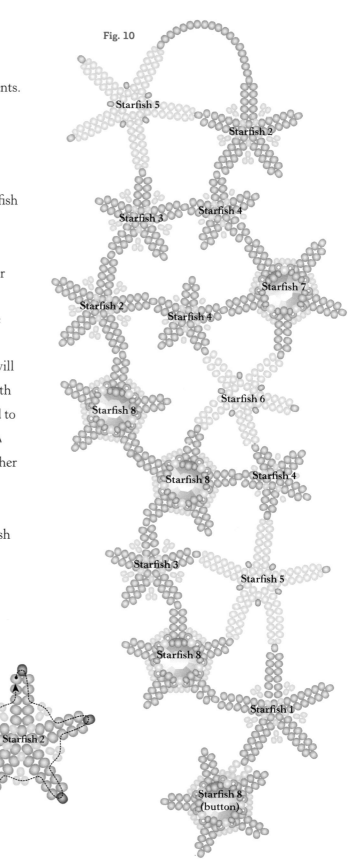

Fig. 10

Starfish 5

Starfish 2

Starfish 3 Starfish 4

Starfish 7

Starfish 2 Starfish 4

Starfish 6

Starfish 8

Starfish 8 Starfish 4

Starfish 3

Starfish 5

Starfish 8

Starfish 1

Starfish 8 (button)

Fig. 11

Starfish 5

Starfish 2

- **STARFISH 1:** Needle up the hanging thread. Pick up 1A and stitch down through 4A. Stitch through the 2C between the arms, then up through the top 4A in the next arm. Repeat four times, omitting A beads and stitching through the A on the tips of neighboring starfish instead for any arms that are used as attachment points; then weave in, secure, and trim the thread **(Fig. 12)**.

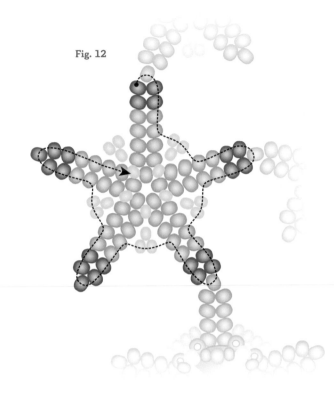

Fig. 12

- **STARFISH 2:** Needle up the working thread. Pick up 1A and stitch down through 3A. Stitch through the 2C between the arms, then up through the top 3A in the next arm. Repeat four times, omitting the addition of A beads and stitching through the A on the tips of neighboring starfish instead for any arms that are used as attachment points; then weave in, secure, and trim the thread.

- **STARFISH 3 AND STARFISH 4:** Needle up the working thread. Pick up 1A and stitch down through 2A. Stitch through the C between the arms, then up through the top 2A in the next arm. Repeat four times, omitting the addition of A beads and stitching through the A on the tips of neighboring starfish instead for any arms that are used as attachment points; then weave in, secure, and trim the thread **(Fig. 13)**.

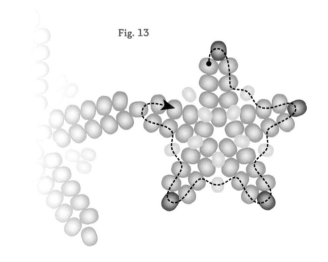

Fig. 13

- **STARFISH 5:** Needle up the working thread. Pick up 1A and stitch down through the next C and 6B. Stitch through the 2D between the arms, then up through the next 6B and first C in the next arm. Repeat four times, omitting the addition of A beads and stitching through the A on the tips of neighboring starfish instead for any arms that are used as attachment points; then weave in, secure, and trim the thread **(Fig. 14)**.

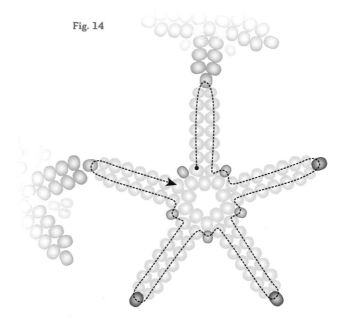

Fig. 14

- **STARFISH 6:** Needle up the working thread. Pick up 1A and stitch down through the next 4B. Stitch through the D between the arms, then up through the next 4B in the next arm. Repeat from the beginning of this step four times, omitting the addition of A beads and stitching through the A on the tips of neighboring starfish instead for any arms that are used as attachment points; then weave in, secure, and trim the thread.

- **STARFISH 7 AND STARFISH 8:** Needle up the working thread. Pick up 1A and stitch down through the next 4A for Starfish 7 or 3A for Starfish 8. Stitch through the 4C between the arms, then up through the top 4A in the next arm. Repeat four times, omitting the addition of A beads and stitching through the A on the tips of neighboring starfish instead for any arms that are used as attachment points; then weave in, secure, and trim the thread **(Fig. 15)**.

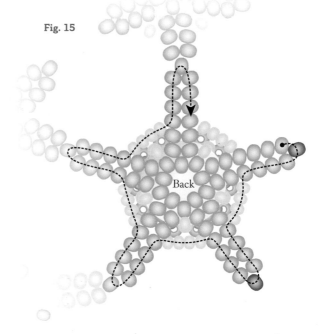

Fig. 15

Back

Tip: If you need to add length to the bracelet or want to change the design, you can stitch extra starfish and attach them to the bracelet as desired.

Attach the Clasp

Fig. 16

35. Return to the Starfish 8 component that you set aside and add A beads to the tip of each arm as instructed in step 34. You will use this component as the button of the clasp. Working on the back side of the starfish, exit from one of the beads in the first round. Pick up 6B. Attach the button to a starfish at one end of the bracelet (in this example, Starfish 1) by stitching through an A at the tip of an unattached arm. Pick up 6B and stitch through an A opposite the first A through which you stitched on the back of Starfish 8. Stitch back through the last 6B added, the A in the tip of Starfish 1, and the next 6B. Stitch through the original A on the back of Starfish 8 **(Fig. 16)**. Repeat the thread path at least twice to reinforce, then weave in, secure, and trim the thread.

36. On the opposite end of the bracelet, secure a new two-foot (61 cm) length of thread to the starfish at the opposite end of the bracelet. In this example, Starfish 5. Exit from the tip of the arm that reaches furthest from the opposite end of the bracelet. Pick up 18A. Attach the 18A to the adjacent starfish (in this case, Starfish 2) by stitching through the tip of an unattached arm **(Fig. 17)**. Before reinforcing, make sure your starfish button fits easily through the loop and holds the bracelet closed. Adjust the bead count, if needed, by undoing the 18A and adding more beads. Retrace the thread path at least twice to reinforce. Weave in, secure, and trim your thread.

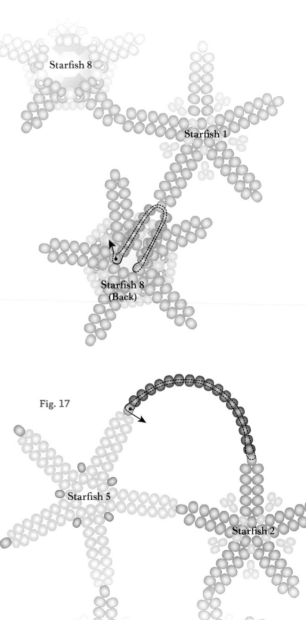

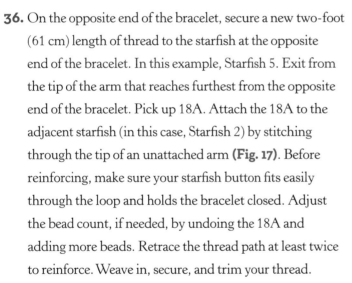

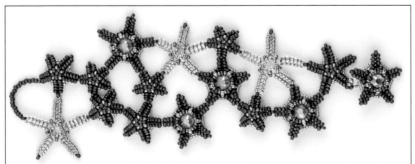

Butterfly Bracelet

After a cold and gray winter, colorful butterfly wings flittering on a meandering path through the air, or a pair of butterflies dancing around each other across the yard, are heartwarming sights. The design of this bracelet is based on their strikingly vivid coloration and bold wing patterning.

TECHNIQUES

Tubular herringbone stitch (page 9)

Tubular peyote stitch (page 7)

Netting (page 8)

Ladder stitch (page 8)

Symbols

▢ A   ◯ D
● B   ◯ E
◯ C   ◯ F

INSTRUCTIONS

Make the Right-Hand Bezels

1. Needle up a wingspan of thread and pick up 30A. Stitch through the first 3A again to form a loop. Leave a tail thread just long enough to weave into the beadwork later and secure. For the Right-Hand Bezels, the butterfly wing will be on the right side.

2. Work one round of peyote stitch using 1A in each stitch to add a total of 15A. Step up through the first A added (**Fig. 1, pink thread**).

    Tip: Use low to medium thread tension to construct the bezel until you add the final round of D on the front and back sides of the bezel in step 5. This will allow you to avoid breaking any beads and pass through the rounds of A and B again without too much trouble.

3. Work one round peyote stitch using 1C for each stitch to add a total of 15C. Step up through the first C added (**Fig. 1, blue thread**).

4. Work one round of peyote stitch using 1D for each stitch to add a total of 15D (**Fig. 1, black thread**).

Fig. 1

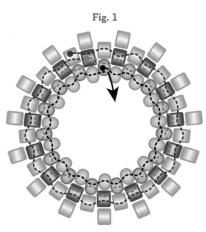

SKILL LEVEL

Advanced intermediate

DIMENSIONS

7 1/2 inches (19.1 cm) long and 1 1/4 inches (3.2 cm) wide

Each additional component beyond the eight shown adds an additional 3/4 inches.

MATERIALS

5 g metallic blue iris size 11° cylinder beads (A)

1 g metallic blue iris size 15° seed beads (B)

1 g stable finish pink opal silver-lined size 15° seed beads (C)

1 g ceylon peach cobbler size 15° seed beads (D)

1 g sea foam luster size 11° seed beads (E)

1 g marbled opaque turquoise/blue size 8° seed beads (F)

9 topaz glacier blue crystal rivolis, 12 mm

8 Pacific opal crystal AB rounds, 3 mm

8 turquoise crystal AB2X rounds, 4 mm

8 turquoise crystal AB2X rounds, 6 mm

Smoke braided fishing line thread, 6 lb

TOOLS

Beader's Tool Kit (page 2)

Size 12 beading needles

5. Weave to the initial loop of the bezel so your thread is emerging from an A in the outermost round. Work one round of peyote stitch using 1C. Step up through the first C added. Place the rivoli faceup in the bezel, then work another round of peyote stitch using 1D for each stitch to add a total of 15D, pulling tightly as you work to encase the rivoli. Do not step up.

6. Stitch through the next 2A **(Fig. 2, blue thread)**. Your thread should emerge from an A in the centermost round of beads.

7. Pick up 1B and 1C and stitch through the next A in the centermost round. Repeat five times, then stitch through the next A in the front-most round of A in the bezel **(Fig. 2, black thread)**.

8. Turn the beadwork over to the back. Reverse your thread direction and stitch through the adjacent A, now the bead above the one through which you just stitched. Stitch through the next A **(Fig. 3, pink thread)**.

9. You will now begin to make the inner sections of the butterfly wing. Pick up 1C and 1B. Stitch through the next A in the same round. Repeat five times, then stitch through the next A in the rearmost round of A in the bezel **(Fig. 3, black thread)**.

10. Turn the beadwork over to the front. Reverse direction and stitch through the adjacent A (the bead above the one from which your thread is emerging). Stitch through the next A in the bezel and the B after it **(Fig. 4, blue thread)**. Pick up 1B and 1C, then stitch through the next C to complete a herringbone stitch. Pass up through the next B. Repeat from the beginning of this step five times. When working the fifth repeat, you will stitch through just the next C after picking up the new beads **(Fig. 4, black thread)**.

11. Turn the beadwork over to the back. Stitch up through the adjacent C on the back side of the bezel. Pick up 1C and 1B, then stitch down through the next B and up through the next C. Repeat from the beginning of this step five times. When working the fifth repeat, you will stitch through just the next B after picking up the new beads **(Fig. 5)**.

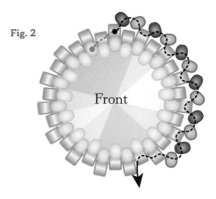

Fig. 2 — Front

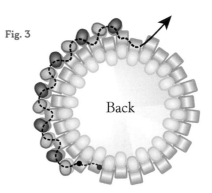

Fig. 3 — Back

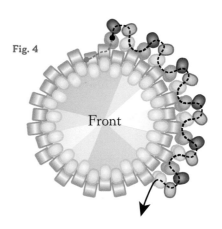

Fig. 4 — Front

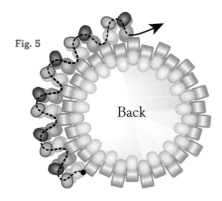

Fig. 5 — Back

12. Turn the beadwork over to the front. Stitch through the adjacent B on the front of the bezel, then step up through the next B.

   Pick up 1A and 1C. Stitch through the next C in the previous row. Pick up 1D and stitch through the B on the top of the next ladder. Repeat from the beginning of this step four times. When working the fourth repeat, you will stitch through just the next C after picking up the new beads **(Fig. 6)**.

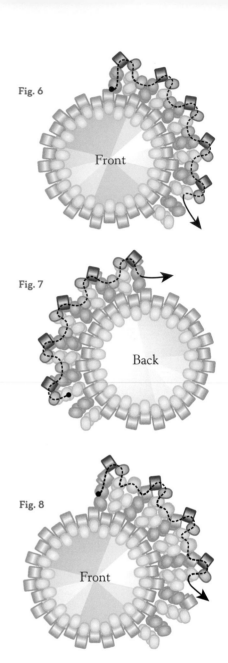

Fig. 6

Front

Fig. 7

Back

13. Turn the beadwork over to the back. Reverse direction and stitch through the adjacent C.

   Pick up 1C and 1A and stitch through the next B in the previous row. Pick up 1D and stitch through the C on top of the next ladder. Repeat from the beginning of this step four times. When working the fourth repeat, you will stitch through just the next B after picking up the new beads **(Fig. 7)**.

14. Turn the beadwork over to the front. Reverse direction and stitch through the adjacent B, then step up through the next A.

   Pick up 1A and 1C and stitch through the next C in the previous row. Pick up 1E and stitch up through the A on the top of the next ladder. Repeat from the beginning of this step three times. When working the third repeat, you will stitch through just the next C after picking up the new beads **(Fig. 8)**.

Fig. 8

Front

15. Turn the beadwork over to the back. Reverse direction and stitch through the adjacent C.

   Pick up 1C and 1A and stitch through the next A in the previous row. Pick up 1E and stitch through the C on the top of the next ladder. Repeat from the beginning three times. When working the third repeat, you will stitch through just the next A after picking up the new beads **(Fig. 9)**. Turn the beadwork over to the front. Stitch through the adjacent A, then step up through the next A.

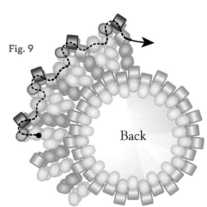

Fig. 9

Back

16. Pick up 1A and 1C and stitch through the next C in the previous row **(Fig. 10)**. Turn the beadwork over to the back again. Reverse direction and stitch through the adjacent C. Pick up 1C and 1A and stitch through the next A in the previous row **(Fig. 11)**. Return to the front of the beadwork. Reverse direction and stitch through the adjacent A, then step up through the next A.

17. Repeat step 16 three more times for a total of eight rows in this herringbone tube. After you complete the eighth row and step up, continue working on the front side and stitch down through the next 6C in the ladder. Stitch through the next E and up through the top 2A in the next ladder **(Fig. 12)**.

18. Repeat step 16 three times for a total of seven rows in the second herringbone tube. Stitch down through the next 5C, the next E, and up through the top 2A in the next ladder **(Fig. 13)**.

19. Repeat step 16 once to add one row to the third herringbone tube. After adding the last 1C and 1A, do not move back to the front of the tube. Instead stitch down one more A, then through the next E, moving toward the second herringbone tube. Stitch up through the next 5C, down through the next 5A, the next E, up through the next 6C, and down through the next A **(Fig. 14)**. You have now completed the inner sections of the butterfly wing. Turn the beadwork over to the front to start working on the outer structure of the wing.

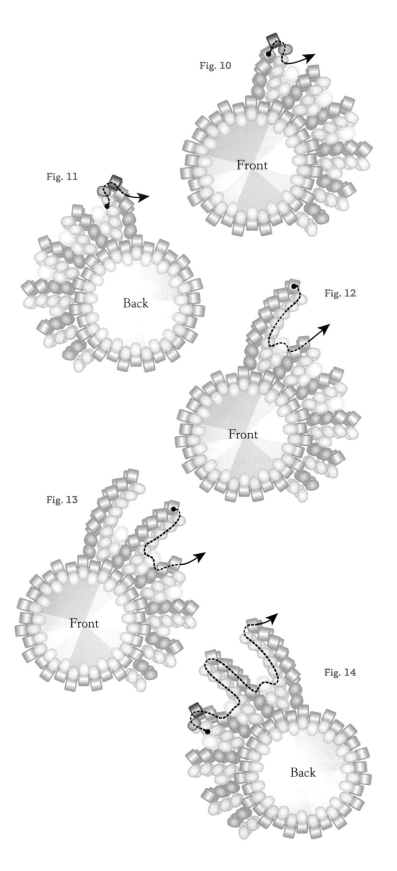

Fig. 10

Fig. 11

Front

Back

Fig. 12

Front

Fig. 13

Front

Fig. 14

Back

32. You'll now fill in the structure of the butterfly wing with seed beads and crystals. Pick up 1E. Moving in a counterclockwise direction, stitch through the top C in the next herringbone tube and the next B **(Fig. 23, brown thread)**.

33. Pick up 1F. Stitch through the top C in the next herringbone tube, away from the bezel. Stitch through the next A, moving toward the bezel **(Fig. 23, pink thread)**.

34. Pick up one 3-mm round. Stitch through the top C in the next herringbone tube, away from the bezel. Stitch through the next A, moving toward the bezel **(Fig. 23, green thread)**.

35. Pick up one 4-mm round. Stitch through the top C in the next herringbone tube, away from the bezel. Stitch through the next A, moving toward the bezel **(Fig. 23, blue thread)**.

36. Pick up one 6-mm round. Stitch through the top C in the next herringbone tube, away from the bezel. Stitch through the next A, moving toward the bezel **(Fig. 23, black thread)**.

37. Turn the beadwork over to the back. Reverse direction and stitch through the adjacent A to bring your thread to the back of the bezel, then stitch through the next C. Retrace the thread path outlined in steps 32–36, starting from the 6-mm round and working backwards until you stitch through the B in the top row of the last herringbone tube **(Fig. 24, blue thread)**.

38. Working only on the back side, stitch through the B beads in the folded ladders, then stitch through the next A **(Fig. 24, black thread)**.

39. Turn the beadwork over to the front. Reverse direction and stitch through the adjacent A to bring your thread to the front side of the bezel, then stitch through the next 3C. Pick up 3B and, heading away from the bezel, stitch through the third A down from the top of the next herringbone ladder and the next C. Pick up 2B and, heading away from the bezel, stitch through the second A down from the top in the next herringbone ladder **(Fig. 25)**. If you have at least 12 inches (30.5 cm) of working thread, leave it hanging for assembly. Weave in, secure, and trim the tail thread.

40. Repeat steps 1–39 three more times for a total of four Right-Hand Bezels.

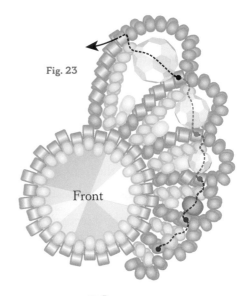

Fig. 23

Front

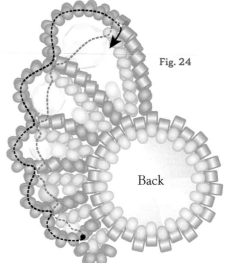

Fig. 24

Back

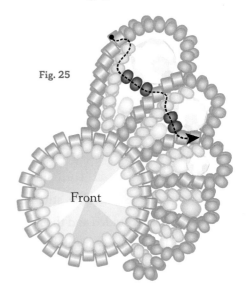

Fig. 25

Front

Make the Left-Hand Bezels

41. To make a Left-Hand Bezel, follow steps 1–39 with the following adjustment to ensure that the butterfly wing will be on the left side. When you start step 7, make sure you are working in the opposite direction as you did for the Right-Hand Bezels. For example, if you worked step 7 in a clockwise fashion for the Right-Hand Bezels, work it in a counterclockwise fashion for the Left-Hand Bezels.

Make the Button Bezel

42. Follow steps 1–5, then weave to a D on the back side of the bezel. Weave in, secure, and trim the tail thread.

43. Pick up 7D and, in the bezel, stitch through the fifth D away from the first D at which you started. Repeat from the beginning of this step twice to add two more groups of 7D around the back of the bezel. Step up through the first 4D added this row **(Fig. 26, blue thread)**.

44. Stitch through the middle D in the next group of 7D and the middle D in the next group of 7D, then stitch through the middle D in the first group of 7D once more **(Fig. 26, black thread)**. Reinforce this thread path once. Leave your thread hanging for assembly.

Assembly

45. Line up the Left-Hand Bezels and Right-Hand Bezels in a column, alternating between each type of bezel. Set the Button Bezel aside for now. You will use the hanging thread on each bezel or start a new 12-inch (30.5 cm) length of thread to attach the bezels to each other.

46. On the first bezel, weave through the beadwork until your thread emerges from the third B on the front side of the shortest folded-over ladder. This bead is the one marked with a dot at the beginning of the thread path in **Figure 27**.

47. Working only with beads on the front side of the bezel, pick up 1B and stitch through the fourth A away from the start of the first herringbone tube in the next bezel. Pick up 1B and stitch through the second and third B on the shortest folded-over ladder of the first bezel **(Fig. 27)**.

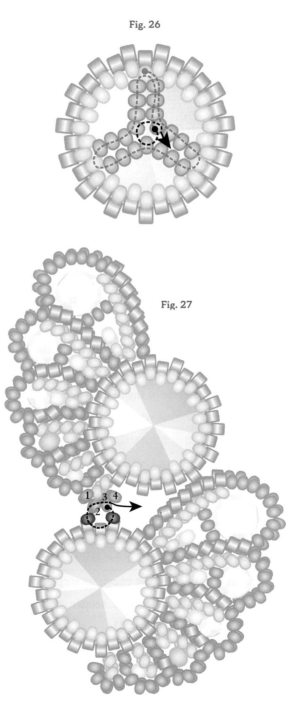

Fig. 26

Fig. 27

Metaphase Bracelet

I can remember the first time I saw illustrations and photos of mitosis, or the process of cell division, in high school biology class. When a cell divides, its chromosomes are copied and line up along the center of a cell. During metaphase, the middle stage of mitosis, spindle fibers connected to each side of the cell pull the pairs of chromosomes apart. This bracelet is inspired by drawings of those spindle fibers stretching from one side of the cell to the other in a beautiful array of arcs. The lemon fancy crystal stones in this bracelet mirror the shape of those fibers, and the circular components that house the stones echo the cells that contain them.

INSTRUCTIONS

Make the Lemon Stone Bezels

1. Needle up a wingspan and a half of thread and pick up 42A. Stitch through the first three beads again to form a loop, leaving an 18-inch tail (45.7 cm) **(Fig. 1, purple thread)**. Pick up 1A, skip the next A, and stitch through the two after it to create a modified peyote stitch. Repeat the modified peyote stitch 13 times, then step up through the first A added **(Fig. 1, blue thread)**.

2. Work a round of peyote stitch, using 2C for each stitch. Step up through the first pair of C added **(Fig. 1, pink thread)**.

SKILL LEVEL

Advanced intermediate

DIMENSIONS

7¹/₂ inches (19 cm) long and 1¹/₂ inches (3.8 cm) wide

MATERIALS

4 g nickel-plated size 11o cylinder beads (A)

2 g white-lined teal AB size 11o cylinder beads (B)

8 g palladium-plated size 15o seed beads (C)

2 g galvanized champagne gold size 15o seed beads (D)

81 golden shadow/silver crystal rose montées, SS12/PP24

84 dove gray crystal pearls, 4 mm

5 aquamarine glacier crystal lemon fancy stones, 19 × 12 mm

Crystal braided fishing line thread, 6 lb

TOOLS

Beader's Tool Kit (page 2)

Size 12 beading needles

TECHNIQUES

Tubular peyote stitch (page 7)

Netting (page 8)

Symbols

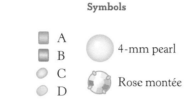

A
B
C
D

4-mm pearl

Rose montée

Fig. 1

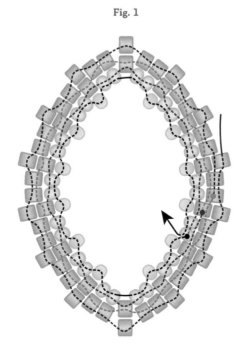

3. Pick up 1D and stitch through the next pair of C added in the previous round. Repeat twice. Skip the next space by stitching directly into the next pair of C added previously. Pull tightly so the beadwork bends into a corner. It's very important to pull as tightly as you can, especially when skipping spaces, to maintain the shape of the corner. Pick up 1D and stitch through the next pair of C in the previous round. Repeat five times. Skip the next space by stitching directly through the next pair of C previously added. Pull tightly so the beadwork bends into a corner. Pick up 1D and stitch through the next pair of C in the previous round. Repeat once. Do not step up **(Fig. 1, black thread)**. Put down the working thread.

4. Needle up the tail thread and stitch through the next 8A. Pick up 1A and stitch through the next pair of A. Make sure the new A is on the back side of the bezel. Stitch through the next A, then reverse direction by stitching through the A in the round below and then back through the pair of A, the new A, and the next pair of A that you passed through earlier. Move your thread to the outside of the beadwork by stitching through the next A **(Fig. 2, blue thread)**. This A is the first of two anchor beads that will be used later to attach the ring component of the bezel.

5. Repeat step 2 **(Fig. 2, pink thread)**.

6. Pick up 1D and stitch through the next pair of C in the round below. Repeat four times. Skip the next space by stitching directly through the next pair of C. Pull tightly so the beadwork bends into a corner. Put a lemon fancy stone in the bezel faceup, lining up the corners of the stone with the corners of the bezel. Holding the stone in place while you work, pick up 1D and stitch through the next pair of C. Repeat five times. Skip the next space by stitching directly through the next pair of C. Pull tightly so the beadwork bends into a corner. Pick up 1D and stitch through the next pair of C **(Fig. 2, black thread)**. If the stone is not already held securely in place or if you cannot tighten the round enough just by pulling the thread, retrace the thread path.

7. Stitch through the adjacent D and next pair of C in the innermost round of beads on the front of the bezel. Repeat three times. Stitch through the next single A and pair of A in the next round so your thread emerges just before the A on the corner of the bezel. Pick up 1A and stitch through the next pair of A, making sure the new A sits in the skipped space, or ditch. Stitch through the next single A on the top round **(Fig. 3, pink thread)**. Reverse direction by stitching through the A directly beneath it. Stitch back through the pair of

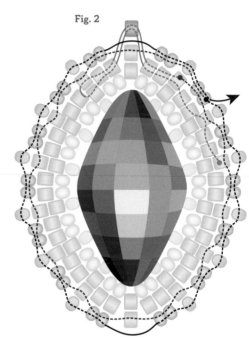

Fig. 2

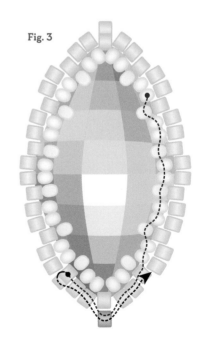

Fig. 3

A and the newly added A, then the next pair of A that you passed through earlier **(Fig. 3, black thread)**. Weave in, secure, and trim the thread.

8. Turn the bezel over to the back and needle up the working thread that you had put down in step 3. Stitch through the next D, which should be the second one from the corner of the bezel. *Pick up 3D, 1B, and 3D; skip the next 2D in the bezel round and stitch through the third. Repeat from * three times, then step up through the first 3D and B added **(Fig. 4, pink thread)**.

9. Pick up 2C and stitch through the next B. Repeat three times **(Fig. 4, black thread)**.

10. Stitch through the next 4D, the next pair of C, then the A in the bezel round in the direction toward the corner of the bezel. Continue stitching through A until your thread emerges from the A added in the ditch at the corner **(Fig. 5)**.

11. Repeat steps 1–10 four more times for a total of five lemon stone bezels.

Make the Rings

12. You will now make the ring on the outside of the bezel. Pick up seven repeats of [3C, 1A], then 3C. Stitch through the A in the ditch at the opposite bezel corner. Repeat from the beginning of this step once **(Fig. 6, purple thread)**.

13. Pick up 3C and stitch through the next A in the previous round. Repeat all the way around the ring of beads, including the A in the ditch at the opposite corner. Pull tightly as you go so that the groups of 3C sit on top or below the 3C you skip over. Step up through the first group of 3C added **(Fig. 6, blue thread)**.

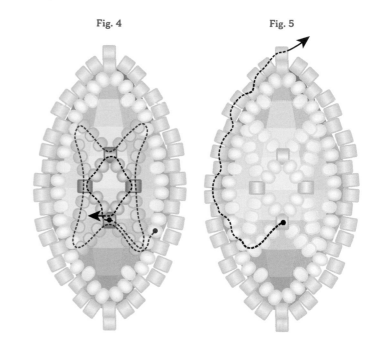

Fig. 4   Fig. 5

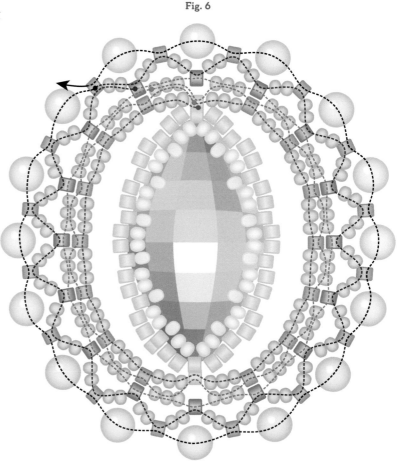

Fig. 6

14. Pick up 1B and stitch through the next group of 3B from the previous round. Repeat all the way around the ring, then step up through the first B added **(Fig. 6, green thread)**.

15. Pick up 2C, 1A, and 2C. Stitch through the next B in the previous round. Repeat fifteen more times, then step up through the first 2C and A added **(Fig. 6, pink thread)**.

16. Pick up one pearl and stitch through the next A in the previous round. Repeat fifteen more times; do not step up **(Fig. 6, black thread)**.

17. Stitch through the next 2C, B, 3C, A, and 3C in the inner rounds so that your thread is emerging from the innermost round of the ring **(Fig. 7)**.

18. You will now work the back side of the ring as the front. Follow step 14 to create the next round **(Fig. 8, green thread)**.

19. Follow step 15 to create the next round **(Fig. 8, pink thread)**.

20. Stitch through the next pearl that was added on the front side to zip the two sides of the ring together. Stitch through the next A. Repeat fifteen more times. Do not step up; stitch through the first pearl added **(Fig. 8, blue thread)**.

21. Pick up 3D and stitch through the next pearl. Make sure each group of D sits nicely between the two pearls. Repeat all the way around the ring **(Fig. 8, black thread)**.

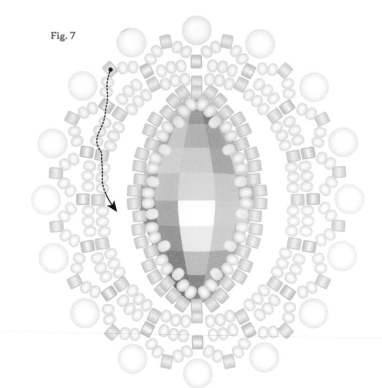

Fig. 7

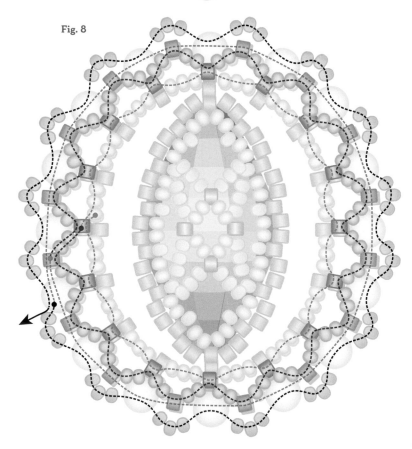

Fig. 8

22. Turn the beadwork over to the front. Stitch through the next A on the front side of the ring, then the next two C and the next B so your thread emerges from the second innermost round **(Fig. 9, pink thread)**.

23. Pick up one rose montée and stitch through the next B. Repeat fifteen more times **(Fig. 9, black thread)**. Weave in, secure, and trim the thread. You have finished one component of the bracelet.

24. Follow steps 12–23 four more times with each remaining lemon stone bezels to create a total of five components. For a 6-inch (15.2 cm) bracelet create only three more components. Add more components as needed for a longer bracelet. Each one adds about 1½ inches (3.8 cm) of length.

Assembly

25. Attach an additional 18 inches (45.7 cm) of thread to the outside rounds of one ring component near one corner of the bezel. Bring your thread out of the pearl that is directly aligned with the corner of the bezel. Working from the back, line up another component in the same orientation next to the first. Pick up 4C and stitch through the pearl at the corner of the second component. Pick up 4C and stitch through the original pearl on the first component to complete a circular thread path **(Fig. 10)**. Make sure the C fall to the back of the components and that the groups of 3D between pearls remain on the front side. Repeat the thread path at least twice to reinforce, pulling the thread tightly to take up any slack. Then weave in, secure, and trim the thread.

26. Repeat step 25 to attach the remaining components together.

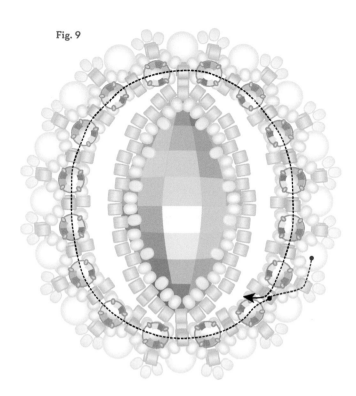

Fig. 9

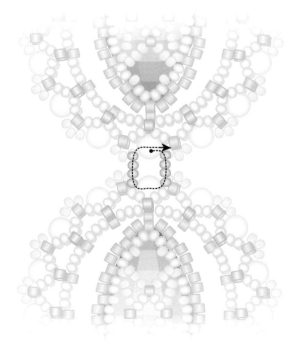

Fig. 10

Make the Closure

27. To create the beaded button, needle up a yard (91.4 cm) of thread and pick up four pearls. Stitch through the first pearl again to form a loop **(Fig. 11, brown thread)**. Repeat the thread path at least once to reinforce.

28. Pick up 1A and stitch through the next pearl. Repeat three more times, then step up through the first A added **(Fig. 11, blue thread)**.

29. Pick up 2C, 1A and 2C. Stitch through the next A in the previous round. Repeat three more times, then step up through the first 2C and A added in this round **(Fig. 11, pink thread)**.

30. Pick up 1D and stitch through the next A. Repeat three more times, pulling tightly to bring the A together over the center of the pearls **(Fig. 11, black thread)**.

31. Pick up one rose montée and stitch through the A opposite the A from which you started. Stitch back through the rose montée and the first A. Stitch through the next D and A **(Fig. 12, pink thread)**.

32. Stitch through the second hole of the rose montée, making sure it is face up. Stitch through the A opposite the A from which you started, then back through the rose montée and the first A **(Fig. 12, blue thread)**.

33. Stitch through the next 2C and A between pearls **(Fig. 12, black thread)**.

34. Turn the beadwork over to the back. Stitch through the next pearl. *Pick up 1A and stitch through the next pearl. Repeat from * three times, then step up through the first A added **(Fig. 13, blue thread)**.

35. Pick up 6C and stitch through the A directly across from the A from which you started **(Fig. 13, pink thread)**.

36. Pick up 1C and stitch back through the middle 4C in the group of six that you added in the previous step. Pick up 1C and stitch through the first A **(Fig. 13, black thread)**. Reinforce the thread path at least once, and any other thread paths that seem wobbly or that have space between beads, then weave in, secure, and trim the thread.

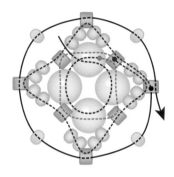

Fig. 11

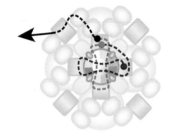

Fig. 12

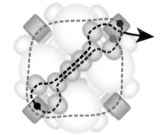

Fig. 13

37. Needle up 24 inches (61 cm) of thread. Weave it into one of the end components of the bracelet by bringing the thread out of the pearl directly in line with the corner of the bezel. Pick up 10C and pass your needle through the loop on the back of the beaded button. Stitch through the same pearl on the end component **(Fig. 14).** Repeat the thread path at least twice to reinforce, making sure to pull the thread tightly to take up any slack.

Fig. 14

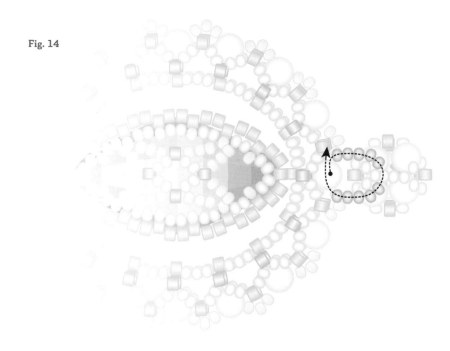

38. To make the loop for the clasp on the other end of the bracelet, needle up 24 inches (61 cm) of thread. Weave it into the other end component of the bracelet by bringing the thread out of an A on the back side of the component, next to the pearl at the corner of the bezel. Pick up 28C and stitch through the A on the opposite side of the pearl, on the back side of the component. Stitch back through the 28C and the first A. Repeat the thread path at least twice, then weave in, secure, and trim the thread.

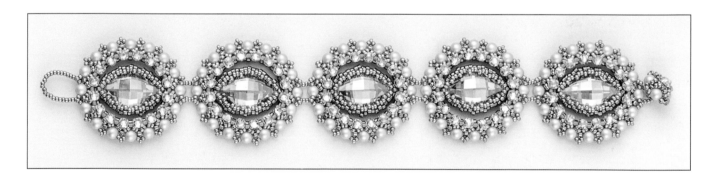

Necklaces

Seed Pod Lariat

There is a plant that grows plentifully along roads and woods in New England called the white campion. It produces small, understated flowers, but the truly beautiful part of the plant is the large, velvety seed pod that forms behind the petals. The shapes, delicate structure, and textures of this elegant lariat are evocative of this gorgeous, fertile seed pod at the base of the blossom. Tubular herringbone stitch combined with netting and right-angle weave combine to produce a simple neck strap and sculptural lariat ends.

INSTRUCTIONS

Make the Embellished Lariat End

1. Needle up one and a half wingspans of thread and pick up 8D. Stitch through the first bead again to form a ring, leaving a tail that is a half wingspan long to work with later.

2. Pick up 2D and stitch through the next bead in the loop. Skip the next two beads and stitch through the third **(Fig. 1, blue thread)**. Repeat to add two more D **(Fig. 1, red thread)**. Stitch through the first bead added in this round to step up **(Fig. 1, green thread)**. Pull the working thread and the tail thread in opposite directions to form two herringbone ladders.

Symbols

- A
- B
- C
- D

3-mm bicone

4-mm bicone

Fig. 1

Ladder 1

Ladder 2

SKILL LEVEL

Low intermediate

DIMENSIONS

39 inches (99.1 cm) long with an 18-inch (45.7 cm) neck loop when doubled over and tied in a knot

MATERIALS

1 g metallic bronze size 15º seed beads (A)

1 g matte gold-lined black diamond size 15º seed beads (B)

1 g metallic bronze size 11º seed beads (C)

20 g matte opaque sea-foam luster size 11º seed beads (D)

16 Pacific opal crystal bicones, 3 mm

48 Pacific opal crystal bicones, 4 mm

4 oxidized bronze two-hole Czech cabochon beads, 6 mm

2 golden shadow ellipse crystal pendants, 32 mm

Nylon beading thread

TOOLS

Beader's Tool Kit (page 2)

Size 12 beading needles

TECHNIQUES

Tubular herringbone stitch (page 9)

Right-angle weave (RAW) (page 10)

Netting (page 8)

3. Pick up 2D and stitch down through the next D. Stitch up through the first D in the second ladder **(Fig. 2)**. Pick up 2D and stitch down through the next D in the ladder **(Fig. 3)**. To step up, stitch through the top 2D in the first ladder **(Fig. 4)**.

4. Repeat step 3 three times to add three more rows of the two-ladder tubular herringbone stitch.

5. To create the lariat end, start by picking up 3A. Stitch down through the second D bead in the first ladder, then stitch up through the first D in the second ladder **(Fig. 5)**.

6. Pick up 3A. Stitch down through the second D in the first ladder, then up through the first D in the second ladder **(Fig. 6)**.

7. Repeat steps 5 and 6 for the remaining two sides of the herringbone tube **(Fig. 7, pink thread)**. Step up through the first 2A in the last group of 3A added **(Fig. 7, black thread)**.

8. Pick up one 3-mm bicone and stitch through the middle A in the next group of 3A. Repeat three times, then step up through the first bicone in this round **(Fig. 8)**.

9. Pick up one C and stitch through the next 3-mm bicone. Repeat three times, then step up through the first C in this round **(Fig. 9)**.

10. Pick up 3A and stitch through the next C in the previous round. Repeat three times, then step up through the first 2A in this round **(Fig. 10)**.

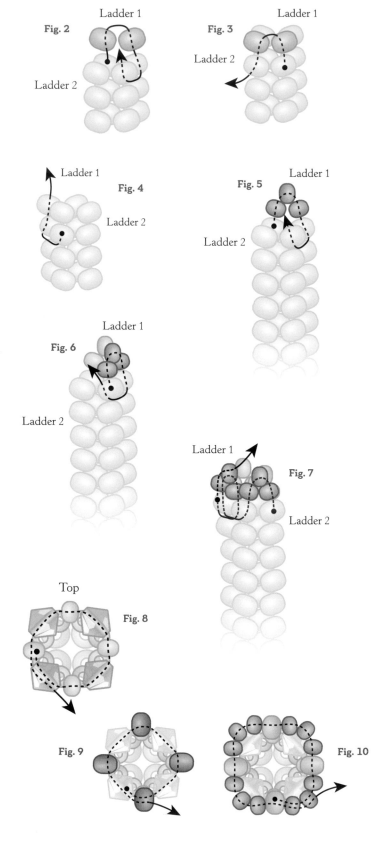

11. Pick up one 4-mm bicone and stitch through the middle A in the next group of 3A from the previous round. Repeat three times, then step up through the first 4-mm bicone in this round **(Fig. 11)**.

12. Pick up 1C and stitch through the next 4-mm bicone in the previous round. Repeat three times, then step up through the first C added **(Fig. 12)**.

13. Pick up 2A, 1C, and 2A. Stitch through the next C from the previous round. Repeat three times, then step up through the first 2A and C in this round **(Fig. 13)**.

14. Orient a two-hole cabochon so that the domed part faces outward. Stitch through the nearest hole of the two-hole cabochon, then pick up 3C and stitch through the other hole of the same cabochon. Stitch through the middle C in the group of 3C added in the previous round. Repeat three times, then step up through the first hole of the first two-hole cabochon in this round and the first C on top of it **(Fig. 14, pink thread)**.

15. Skip the middle C in the group of 3C and stitch through the third C **(Fig. 14, blue thread)**.

16. Pick up one 4-mm bicone. Stitch through the first C in the next group of 3C on top of the cabochon from the previous round, skip the middle C, and stitch through the third C. Repeat three times, pulling the thread tightly as you stitch to bring the cabochons together. Step up through the middle C in the first group of 3C in this round **(Fig. 14, black thread)**.

17. Pick up 6C and a pendant. Stitch through the middle C of the group of 3C directly across the bead, then back through the six new C and the middle C from where you started this step **(Fig. 15, black thread)**. Pull tightly.

18. Stitch again through the first four C in the group of 6Cs **(Fig. 15, blue thread)**.

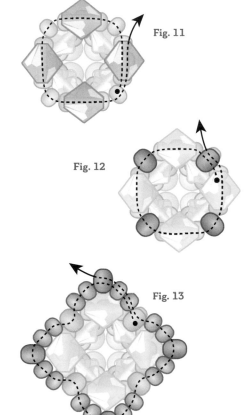

Fig. 11

Fig. 12

Fig. 13

Fig. 14

Fig. 15

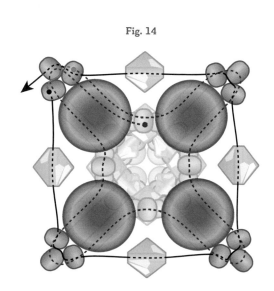

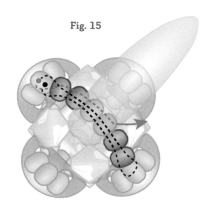

19. Pick up 2C and stitch through the middle
C of the nearest unused group of 3C in the
previous round. Stitch back through the 2C
just added and the middle 2C in the original
group of 6C **(Fig. 16, blue thread)**.

20. Pick up 2C and stitch through the middle C
of the last unused group of 3C in the previous
round. Stitch back through the 2C just added
and the middle 2C in the original group of
6C. Exit through the nearest group of 2C so
that your thread emerges from a middle C in a
group of 3C **(Fig. 16, black thread)**.

*Note: The pendant is not shown in the diagrams from
here on for clarity.*

21. Pick up 5C and stitch through the middle C in the
next group of 3C. Repeat three times, then step up
through the first 3C in this round **(Fig. 17)**.

22. Pick up 3C. Stitch through the C at which you
started this step in a circular fashion to form a RAW
unit, then stitch through the first 2C added. Repeat
twice to create two more RAW units **(Fig. 18, blue
thread)**. Stitch through the second and first RAW
unit to the middle C in the group of 5C. Stitch
through the next 2C in the group of five, the next
C in the previous round, then the next 3C in the
next group of five **(Fig. 18, black thread)**.

23. Repeat step 22 three times to add three more RAW
branches.

24. Stitch through the first C added in the first RAW
unit **(Fig. 19, blue thread)**. Pick up 5B and stitch
through the top 3C in the RAW branch. Pick up
5B and stitch through the C in the first RAW unit
opposite the first. Pick up one 3-mm bicone and
stitch through the first C in the first RAW unit of
the next branch **(Fig. 19, black thread)**.

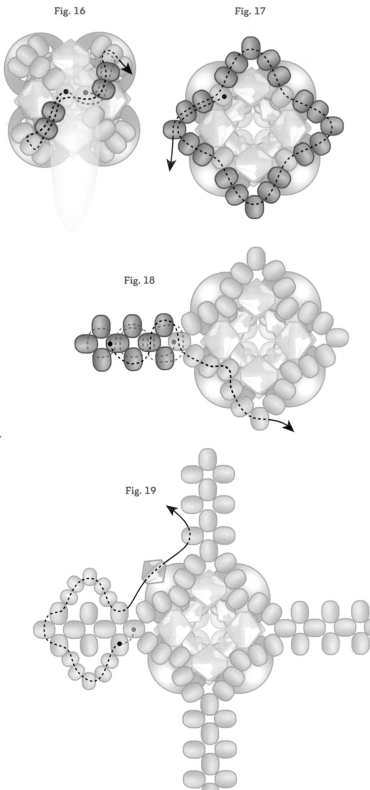

Fig. 16   Fig. 17

Fig. 18

Fig. 19

25. Repeat step 24 three times. Weave in, secure, and trim the working thread.

26. Repeat steps 1–25 to make a second embellished lariat end.

Make the Rest of the Rope

27. Needle up the tail thread to start extending the herringbone rope in the opposite direction of the embellished lariat end. Stitch rows with D until you have 19 rows of the two-ladder tubular herringbone stitch (see step 3).

28. To add an embellishment to the rope, pick up 1A and stitch down through the next D in the first ladder **(Fig. 20, pink thread)**. Pick up 1A and stitch up through the first D in the second ladder **(Fig. 20, black thread)**. Then pick up 1A and stitch up through the second D in the second ladder **(Fig. 21)**. Pick up 1A and stitch up through the first D in the first ladder. Then step up through the first A added **(Fig. 22)**.

29. Pick up 3A and stitch through the next A. Repeat three times, then step up through the first 2A added in the first group of 3A **(Fig. 23)**.

30. Pick up one 3-mm bicone and stitch through the middle A in the next group of 3A. Repeat three times, then step up through the first 3-mm bicone added in this round **(Fig. 24)**.

31. Pick up 1A and stitch through the next 3-mm bicone. Repeat three times, then step up through the first A added in this round **(Fig. 25)**.

32. Pick up 3A and stitch through the next A from the previous round. Repeat three times, then step up through the first 2A added **(Fig. 26)**.

33. Pick up 1D and stitch through the middle A in the next group of 3A in the previous round. Repeat three times, pulling tightly as you go, then step up through the first D in this round **(Fig. 27)**.

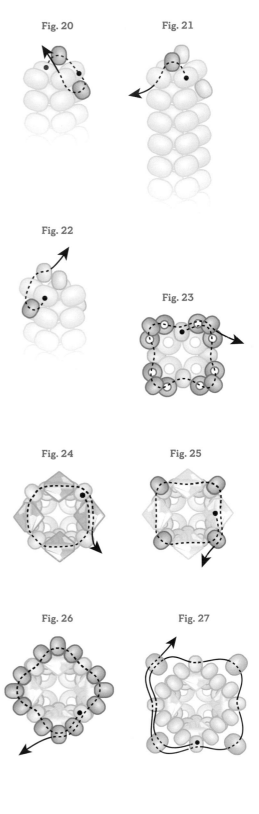

Fig. 20 Fig. 21

Fig. 22

Fig. 23

Fig. 24 Fig. 25

Fig. 26 Fig. 27

34. Resume tubular herringbone by picking up 2D and stitching through the next D in the previous round. Skip over the next A and stitch through the next D. Pick up 2D and stitch through the next D. Skip over the next A and stitch through the next D, then through the first D added in the first pair to step up **(Fig. 28)**.

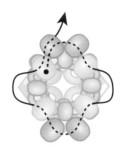

35. Using herringbone stitch to create the rope sections and steps 28–34 to create the embellishment sections, continue adding length to the necklace in the following sequence: a rope section with 44 rows, an embellishment section, a rope section with 56 rows, an embellishment section, a rope section with 74 rows, and an embellishment section. Continue adding more rows of herringbone rope until your lariat is half the desired length of your necklace, about 39 inches (99.1 cm) or more, for a longer necklace.

Fig. 29

36. Repeat steps 27–35 to make a herringbone rope of equal length for the second necklace half.

Assembly

37. Join the two halves of the necklace together using the ends of the herringbone rope. Following the herringbone thread path, stitch back and forth from the end row on one necklace half to the end row on the other **(Fig. 29)**. Weave in, secure, and trim your threads.

Stalactite Necklace

Stalactites are a remarkable feature of the geological world, building up very slowly over time through microscopic deposits of the minerals from drops of water flowing through bedrock and dripping off the ceilings of caves. In this necklace, a stunning partially frosted crystal stone is placed among large hanging crystal pendants and two layers of right-angle weave fringe that pay homage to growing stalactites.

TECHNIQUES

Right-angle weave (RAW) (page 10)

Five-sided prismatic right-angle weave (PRAW-5) (page 13)

Peyote stitch (page 5)

Symbols

● A   ● D
● B   ● E
● C

INSTRUCTIONS

Make the Rope

1. Needle up a wingspan of thread. Create a 15-inch (38.1 cm) long PRAW-5 rope, using 5A for the base and the following sequence of beads for the sides of each unit: [1B, 1A, 1B] for the first side, [1C, 1A] for the second side, [1D, 1A] for the third side, [1C, 1A] for the fourth side, and 1A for the fifth side **(Fig. 1)**. Leave a 12-inch (30.5 cm) tail at the start and your working thread hanging at the end. The sides of the PRAW-5 units with B will be used later to attach the two layers of fringe and the bezel.

Fig. 1

Side   Top

SKILL LEVEL

Intermediate

DIMENSIONS

16 inches (40.6 cm) long and 4 inches (10.2 cm) at widest point

MATERIALS

20 g metallic bronze antique gold size 11o seed beads (A)

10 g metallic bronze size 11o seed beads (B)

2 g matte stable finish galvanized silver size 11o seed beads (C)

2 g stable finish galvanized silver size 11o seed beads (D)

1 g stable finish galvanized silver size 15o seed beads (E)

39 light metallic gold 2X round crystal beads, 4 mm

6 bronze shade partly frosted Crystalactite grand crystal pendants, 30 mm

1 bronze shade partly frosted Crystalactite grand crystal pendant, 56 mm

1 metallic light gold Kaputt oval crystal stone, 29 × 22.5 mm

Smoke braided fishing line thread, 6 lb

TOOLS

Beader's Tool Kit (page 2)

Size 12 beading needles

Make the Back-Fringe Layer

Fig. 2

2. Find the center of the rope by folding it in half. You will make one half of the back-fringe layer at a time. Start a new thread at a spot near the center of the rope, making sure it is secure before weaving it out of one of the B in the centermost PRAW-5 unit. Create a flat chain of RAW off the B using 1A, 1B, and 1A for each unit, for a total of 22 units.

3. With your thread emerging from the last B, pick up 1A, 1B, one 4-mm round, and 3D. Stitch back through the 4-mm round and the B **(Fig. 2, blue thread)**.

4. Pick up 1A. Stitch through the B at the end of the last RAW unit into the side without any thread emerging from it **(Fig. 2, pink thread)**.

5. Begin weaving through the RAW units toward the PRAW-5 rope **(Fig. 2, black thread)**.

6. Once you pass through the B in the PRAW-5 rope, weave over to the corresponding B in the next PRAW-5 unit **(Fig. 3)**.

7. Create another fringe with a total of 22 RAW units. Then weave over to the corresponding B in the next PRAW-5 unit on the rope.

8. Create 14 more fringe pieces on the corresponding B in each PRAW-5 unit of the rope. Each subsequent fringe will be one RAW unit shorter than the one before it; for example, the first fringe added in this step should have 21 RAW units, while the last fringe should have a total of eight RAW units. Make sure each fringe falls along the same line of B in the rope so that the fringe will end up in the back of the necklace. Weave your thread into the rope, secure, and trim any remaining working thread from the fringe.

Fig. 3

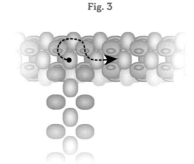

9. To make the other half of the back-fringe layer, start a new wingspan of thread in the center of the necklace. Repeat steps 7 and 8 to create a set of 15 fringe pieces, working from the center point in the opposite direction down the rope and along the same line of B as the first set of fringe. You should now have a total of 31 fringe pieces.

Make the Oval Bezel

10. Needle up a wingspan of thread and pick up 1A, 1B, 1A, and 1B. Stitch through all the beads again to form a loop, leaving just enough of a tail to weave into the beadwork later and trim. Stitch through the first A and B, so your working thread is opposite your tail thread. Create a flat strip of RAW using [1A, 1B, and 1A] for each unit, for a total of 25 units.

11. Add a second row of RAW identical in sequence to the first.

12. Join the beginning and end of the chain together to form a continuous ring: With your thread, which should be emerging from a B on the end of the second row, pick up 1A and stitch through the B at the beginning of the second row. Pick up 1A and stitch through the B at the end of the second row again **(Fig. 4, purple thread).**

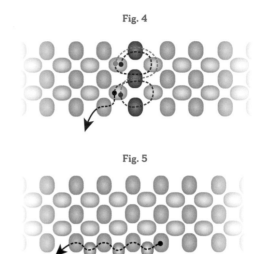

Fig. 4

13. Pass through the next A, B, and A and bring the thread out of the B on the end of the first row **(Fig. 4, blue thread).** Pick up 1A and stitch through the B at the beginning of the first row. Stitch through the A just added between the end and beginning of the second row, then the B at the end of the first row **(Fig. 4, pink thread).** Then stitch through the A on the edge of the first row **(Fig. 4, black thread).** Make sure your ring is not twisted; if it is, undo the join and untwist the RAW strip before rejoining.

Fig. 5

14. Work a row of peyote stitches along the first row of RAW, using 1E for each stitch **(Fig. 5).** Although **Figure 5** only shows three peyote stitches, you should stitch the entire way along the RAW strip. Pull tightly as you work; this will cause the bezel to cup in.

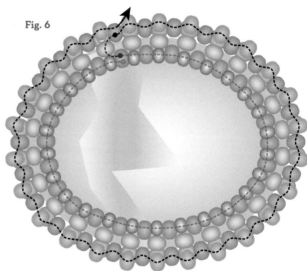

Fig. 6

15. Weave your thread to the outer edge of the second row of RAW. Make peyote stitches along the second row, using 1E for each stitch. Place the oval stone into the bezel faceup as you finish stitching, then pull tightly to hold the stone in place **(Fig. 6, blue thread).**

16. Weave your thread to the nearest A, between the first and second row of RAW **(Fig. 6, pink thread).** Work peyote stitch using 1C for each stitch along the line of A **(Fig. 6, black thread).** Reinforce this row by stitching through all the beads a second time.

17. Orient your stone and bezel based on how you'd like it to appear in the necklace; the jagged facet in the stone can be on the left or the right side when you hang it from the rope. Locate the center C on the bottom side of the bezel. Weave your thread to the fifth C on the left of the center; include the center C in your count. Pick up 2A, 1D, one 30-mm crystal pendant, 1D, and 1A. (Note that the pendant is asymmetrical and can be positioned as desired.) Stitch through the next C, A, C, A, and C in the bezel **(Fig. 7, blue thread).** Pick up 2A, 1B, and 2A. Skip the center C in the bezel and stitch through the next C. Stitch through the next A, C, A, and C **(Fig. 7, pink thread).**

Pick up 1A, 1D, one 30-mm crystal pendant, 1D, and 2A. Stitch through the next C **(Fig. 7, black thread)**. Retrace the thread path through all these beads at least once to reinforce.

18. Stitch through the next eight pairs of A and C to bring your thread out from the C on the right of the center C at the top of the bezel **(Fig. 8, purple thread)**. You will use RAW to attach the bezel to the rope. Line up the PRAW-5 rope so that the center B in front of the fringe is lined up with the center C on the top of the bezel. Pick up 1A and stitch through the B that is right of the center C on the rope. Pick up 1A and stitch through the first C, the next A, and center B in the PRAW-5 rope to complete one RAW unit **(Fig. 8, blue thread)**. Make two more RAW units in this manner to finish attaching the bezel **(Fig. 8, pink and black threads)**. Retrace the thread path at least once to reinforce. Weave in, secure, and trim your thread.

Attach the Large Pendant

19. Needle up a half wingspan of thread. You'll create a bead cap for the top of the pendant before attaching it to the oval bezel. Follow step 10, but create only nine units. Join the ninth unit to the first unit by following step 12. Bring your thread out of an A.

20. Work a row of peyote stitch along one edge of the loop, using 1C for each stitch **(Fig. 9)**. Step up through the first C added.

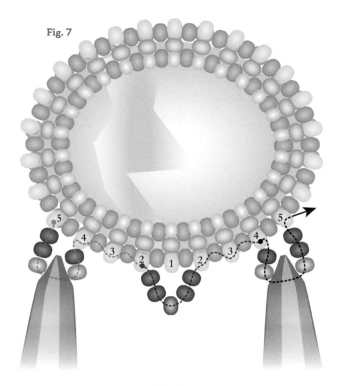

Fig. 7

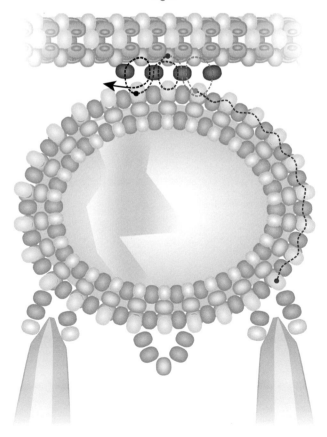

Fig. 8

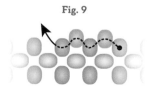

Fig. 9

21. Work another row of peyote stitch, this time using 1A for each stitch **(Fig. 10)**. Step up through the first A added.

22. Pick up 1B, 1C, and 1B. Skip the next A and stitch through the following A **(Fig. 11)**. Repeat four times, then step up through the first B and C added.

23. Pick up 2A and stitch through the next C **(Fig. 12)**. Repeat four times, then step up through the first 2A added.

24. Work one row of peyote stitch with 1B for each stitch, passing through both A in each pair added in the previous round **(Fig. 13)**. Step up through the first B added.

25. Pick up 2A and stitch through the next B **(Fig. 14)**. Repeat four times, then step up through the first 2A added.

26. Pick up 3A, skip the next 4A and stitch through the third pair. Pick up 2A, skip the next pair of A, and stitch through the following pair **(Fig. 15, pink thread)**. Retrace the thread path at least once, then step up through the first two A in the group of three just added **(Fig. 15, black thread)**.

27. You will now make a beaded loop that goes through the loop on the bottom of the bezel. Pick up 2A, 1B, and 2A. Move the needle and thread through the loop at the bottom of the oval bezel, without passing through any beads, then stitch through an A in the pair added in the previous step. Stitch back through the 2A, B, and 2A just added, then through the middle A in the group of 3A added in the previous step **(Fig. 16)**. Make sure the thread does not catch between the beads on the bezel loop, then tighten the thread. Retrace the thread path at least twice to reinforce.

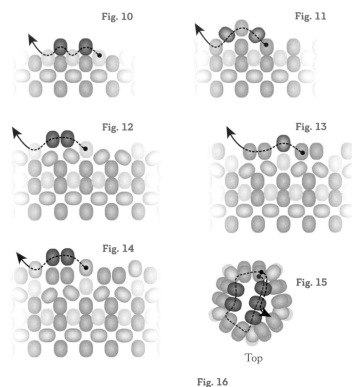

Fig. 10

Fig. 11

Fig. 12

Fig. 13

Fig. 14

Fig. 15

Top

Fig. 16

28. Stitch down four rows to the one made from groups of B, C, B in step 22. Bring your thread out of a C. Stitch through the hole of the 56-mm crystal pendant and a C in the same row on the opposite side of the beadwork. Pull tightly to move the top of the pendant into the cupped beadwork. Stitch back and forth through the 2C at least two more times. If your beads fill up with too much thread to do this, then stitch back and forth through nearby beads at least two more times. Weave in, secure, and trim your working thread and tail thread.

Make the Front-Fringe Layer

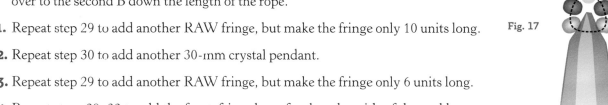

29. Like the back-fringe layer, you will make one half of the front-fringe layer at a time. Start a new wingspan of thread in the PRAW-5 rope to the right of the oval stone bezel. Bring it out of the third B from the nearest connection point to the bezel on the front side of the rope. Create a fringe using RAW with the following sequence of beads for each unit: [1A, 1C, 1A] for 14 units total. Follow steps 3 and 4 to make the end of the fringe, substituting C for B. Weave back up the RAW to the B in the PRAW-5 rope.

30. Weave to the second B down the length of the rope in the front row of B. Create one RAW unit with the following sequence of beads: 1A, 1C, 1A **(Fig. 17, pink thread)**. Pick up 1A, 1D, one 30-mm crystal pendant, 1D, and 1A. Stitch through the C in the RAW unit **(Fig. 17, black thread)**. Make sure the pendant is oriented the way you want it; if not, just take the pendant off and reattach it. Stitch through the beads just added again to reinforce, then weave up to the B in the PRAW-5 rope where you started and over to the second B down the length of the rope.

31. Repeat step 29 to add another RAW fringe, but make the fringe only 10 units long.

Fig. 17

32. Repeat step 30 to add another 30-mm crystal pendant.

33. Repeat step 29 to add another RAW fringe, but make the fringe only 6 units long.

34. Repeat steps 29–33 to add the front-fringe layer for the other side of the necklace.

Make the Toggle Bar

35. To create the toggle bar for the necklace closure, needle up a half wingspan of thread. Leaving a 16-inch (40.6 cm) tail, create a PRAW-5 rope five units long, using 5A for the base and the following sequence of beads for the remaining sides of each unit: [1B, 1A, 1B] for the first side, [1C, 1A] for the second side, [1D, 1A] for the third side, [1C, 1A] for the fourth side, and 1A for the fifth side. Put down the working thread for now and needle up the tail thread. Create one additional PRAW-5 unit off the tail side, for a total of six units, making sure the bead color pattern stays the same.

36. Weave around to bring your thread out of the D in the last PRAW-5 unit on the opposite end of the rope. Pick up one 4-mm round and stitch down into one of the 2B in the unit **(Fig. 18, black thread)**. Stitch through the next A in the unit, then out of the second B in the unit. Stitch back through the 4-mm round and into the D **(Fig. 18, pink thread)**.

37. Bring the thread out of an A at the end of the unit. Work peyote stitch around the unit, using 2E for each stitch **(Fig. 19)**. Weave in, secure, and trim the thread.

38. Needle up the working thread again. Repeat steps 36 and 37 to add a 4-mm round to the other end of the PRAW-5 rope. To strengthen the toggle bar, stitch again through the 5A on the tops and bottoms of each PRAW-5 unit, working from one side of the toggle bar to the other. Weave in, secure, and trim the thread.

39. Needle up the hanging thread on one end of the necklace. Work a round of peyote stitch, using 1E for each stitch. With your thread emerging from an A, pick up 7A and stitch through the center A between the rows of B on the toggle bar. Pick up 7A and stitch through the A opposite to the A where you started on the end of the necklace **(Fig. 20)**. Stitch back through the last 7A, the B in the toggle bar, and the next 7A, then through the original A in the necklace. Retrace the thread path at least twice to reinforce. Weave in, secure, and trim the thread.

Make the Toggle Loop

40. Needle up a half wingspan of thread and pick up 1A, 1B, 1A, and 1B. Stitch through all the beads again to form a loop, leaving just enough of a tail to weave into the beadwork later and trim. Stitch through the first A and B so your working thread is opposite your tail thread. Create a flat strip of RAW, using the following sequence: [1A, 1B, 1A] for a total of fifteen units. Add a second row of RAW identical in sequence to the first. Then follow steps 12 and 13 to join the ends of the RAW strip to form a continuous ring.

41. Work one row of peyote stitch on one edge of the RAW cylinder, using 1E for each stitch. Pull tightly as you go.

42. Weave your thread to the other edge and work one row of peyote stitch, using 1E for each stitch. Pull tightly as you go. Step up through the first E added **(Fig. 21, blue thread)**. Work another row of peyote stitch, using 1E for each stitch. Again, pull tightly as you go, and step up **(Fig. 21, black thread)**.

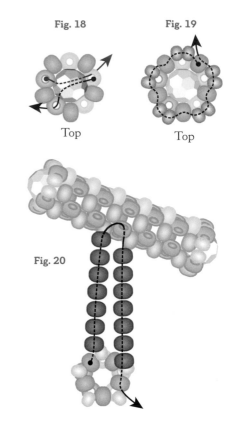

Fig. 18   Fig. 19

Top   Top

Fig. 20

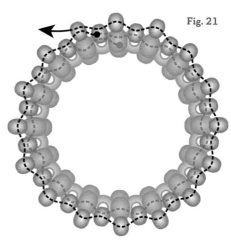

Fig. 21

43. Stitch alternately through the beads in the first row of E on the other side of the RAW cylinder and the beads in the row of E added in previous step to zip the two sides of the RAW cylinder together to form the toggle loop **(Fig. 22)**. To access the holes of the beads as you stitch, you may have to pass the needle back and forth through the toggle loop itself.

44. Once completely zipped, weave your thread to the outside edge of the toggle loop, which should be the row of A at the center of the original RAW cylinder. Work peyote stitch, using 2E for each stitch, all the way around the loop. Weave in, secure, and trim the thread.

45. Needle up the hanging thread on the unfinished end of the necklace. Work a round of peyote stitch using 1E for each stitch. With your thread emerging from an A, pick up 4A and stitch through an A along the outside edge of the toggle loop. Pick up 4A and stitch through an A across from the A where you started on the end of the necklace **(Fig. 23)**. Stitch back through the 4A, the A on the toggle loop, then the startinf A. Retrace the thread path at least twice to reinforce. Weave in, secure, and trim the thread.

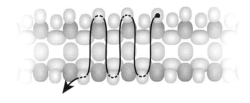

Fig. 22

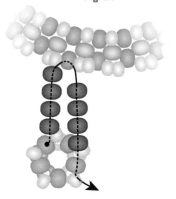

Fig. 23

Orchid Necklace

The flowers in this necklace are based on the shape of moth orchids, whose blossoms are known for their intricate center folds, brightly patterned coloring, and stunning mix of symmetry and asymmetry. Something about that large, precisely folded flower on a long, delicate stalk is magical. This necklace uses a combination of peyote stitch and netting with cylinder beads and seed beads to create sculptured, life-like petals with a gradation of color.

Note: Nylon thread is highly recommended for stitching the petals because you will pass the thread through the seed beads many times. Using fishing line instead will cause the beads to break or fill up with thread faster. Nylon also provides more flexibility when you weave through the matrix of peyote stitched cylinder beads to create each petal. For stitching the stem as well as the chain and toggle, I recommend fishing line thread to give them more structural stability and strength.

INSTRUCTIONS

Make the Orchids

Make the Large Petals

1. Needle up a wingspan of nylon thread. Pick up 12F, 1E and 1F. Stitch back through the third to last bead, forming a picot (three beads in a triangular configuration) consisting of 1F, 1E, and 1F. Leave the tail thread just long enough to weave into the beadwork later and trim. Work five peyote stitches, using 1F for each stitch **(Fig. 1, blue thread)**. This is Row 1.

2. For Row 2, pick up 1C. Working in the direction toward the tip of the petal, or towards the picot, stitch back through the last F added in the previous row. Work one peyote stitch with 1C and four peyote stitches with 1E for each

SKILL LEVEL

Advanced

DIMENSIONS

17 1/2 inches (44.5 cm) long with 3-inch (7.6 cm) diameter flowers

MATERIALS

5 g metallic 24-karat gold size 15o seed beads (A)

3 g matte silver-lined lavender size 15o seed beads (B)

8 g ceylon light purple size 11o cylinder beads (C)

2 g luminous plum crazy size 11o cylinder beads (D)

2 g ceylon white size 11o cylinder beads (E)

12 g matte transparent rainbow lime size 11o seed beads (F)

3 tanzanite top-drilled crystal pear-shaped pendants, 22 mm

Nylon beading thread for stitching the petals

Braided fishing line thread, 6 lb, for stitching the stem, chain, and toggle

TOOLS

Beader's Tool Kit (page 2)

Size 12 or 13 beading needles

TECHNIQUES

Peyote stitch (page 5)

Netting (page 8)

Symbols

◯ A	◻ D
◯ B	◻ E
◻ C	◯ F

Fig. 1

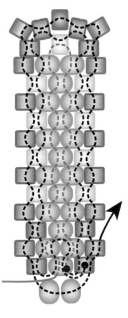

stitch. At the tip of the petal, work two peyote stitches using 2D for each stitch. The 2D should fall between the F and the E from the previous row. Work four peyote stitches using 1E for each stitch and work one peyote stitch using 1C. Pick up 1C and reverse direction, stitching through the adjacent F at the very bottom of the petal. Then stitch through the next F, reverse direction, and stitch through the adjacent F, then stitch through the F at the very bottom of the petal again. Step up through the first C added in this row **(Fig. 1, red thread)**.

3. Working toward the petal tip, start Row 3 with five peyote stitches, using 1D for each stitch. Work five more peyote stitches at the tip of the petal, using 1C for each stitch, then add five additional peyote stitches, using 1D for each stitch. Pick up 2F and stitch through the nearest C on the other side of the bottom F. Working toward the tip of the petal, step up through the first D added in this row **(Fig. 1, black thread)**.

4. For Row 4, stitch through the adjacent F away from the tip of the petal, then through the next C. Reverse direction and pick up 1C, then stitch through the next D. Work six peyote stitches, using 1C in each stitch. At the tip of the petal, *pick up 2C and stitch through the C in the previous row. Repeat from * once, then work six peyote stitches using 1C for each stitch. Add one final C, then reverse direction and stitch through the adjacent C to start an odd-count thread path **(Fig. 2, blue thread)**. Complete the odd-count thread path to bring your thread out of the new C that you just added **(Fig. 2, red thread)**. Pick up 1F and stitch through the pair of F on the petal base. Pick up 1F and step up through the first C added in this row **(Fig. 2, black thread)**.

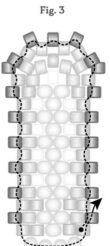

Fig. 2

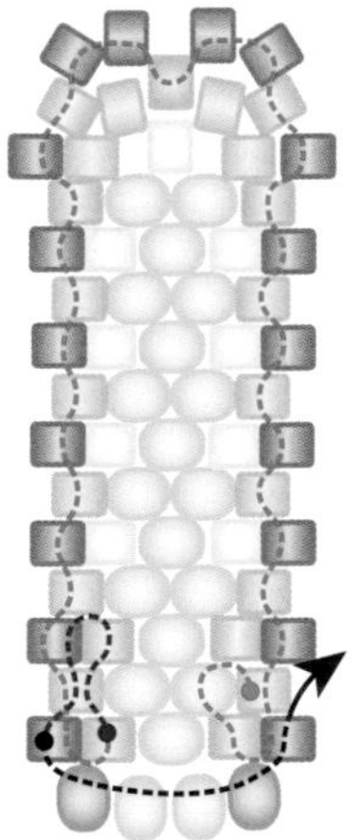

5. For Row 5, work six peyote stitches, using 1C for each stitch. When you approach the tip of the petal, pick up 2C, then stitch through the next C in the previous row. Pick up 1C, then stitch through the next C in the previous row. Work one peyote stitch using 1C. Pick up 1C, then stitch through the next C in the previous row. Pick up 2C, stitch through the next C in the previous row, and work six peyote stitches using 1C for each stitch. Stitch through the 4F at the base of the petal. Step up through the first C added in this row **(Fig. 3)**.

6. For Row 6, work six peyote stitches, using 1C for each stitch; when adding the sixth stitch, pass through the pair of C in the previous row as if they're one bead. At the tip of the petal, work four peyote stitches using 1C for each stitch; after adding the fourth stitch, pass through the pair of C in the previous row as if they're one bead. Work six more peyote stitches, using 1C for each stitch, then stitch through the next C and the 4F at the bottom of the petal. Step up through the first C added in this row **(Fig. 4)**.

Fig. 3

Fig. 4

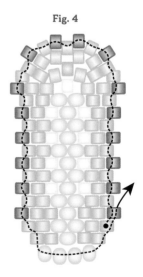

7. For Row 7, work five peyote stitches using 1C for each stitch. Pick up 3C and stitch through the next C in the previous row, making sure the 3C (shown with black outlines in **Figure 5**) fall into the space with the 2C two rows back. For the next space, pick up 2C and stitch through the next C in the previous row. Work one peyote stitch with 1C. For the next space, pick up another 2C and stitch through the next C in the previous row. Pick up 3C and stitch through the next C in the previous row, making sure the 3C (shown with black outlines in **Figure 5**) fall into the space with the 2C two rows back. Work five peyote stitches, using 1C for each stitch. Finish the row by stitching through the next 2C, the 4F at the bottom of the petal, and then the next 4C to step up through the first C added in this row **(Fig. 5, green thread)**.

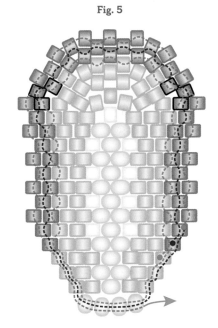

Fig. 5

8. For Row 8, work five peyote stitches, using 1C for each stitch; after adding the fifth stitch, pass through the group of three C in the previous row. Work one peyote stitch with 1C, stitching through just the first C in the next pair of C in the previous row. Work another peyote stitch with 1C, stitching through the second C in the pair. Work two more peyote stitches, using 1C for each stitch; to complete the second stitch, pass only through the first C in the next pair of C in the previous row. Work one peyote stitch with 1C, passing through the second C in the pair. Work one peyote stitch with 1C, passing through the group of 3C added in the previous row. Work five peyote stitches, using 1C for each stitch, then stitch through the next 3C, the next 4F at the bottom of the petal, and the next 5C to step up through the first C added in the row **(Fig. 5, red thread)**.

9. For Row 9, work four peyote stitches using 1C for each stitch. *For the next stitch, pick up 1C and stitch through the middle C in the next group of 3C. Then pick up 1C and stitch through the next C in the previous row. Work five peyote stitches using 1C for each stitch. Repeat from * once. Stitch through the next 4C and the next 4F at the bottom of the petal **(Fig. 5, blue thread)**.

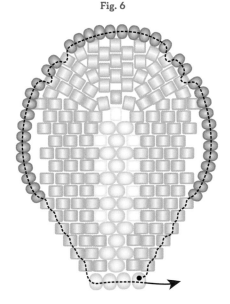

Fig. 6

10. For Row 10, stitch through the 6C on the edge in the direction toward the petal tip. Pick up 12B and stitch through the fifth C away from where your thread was emerging in Row 9. Pick up 2B and stitch through the next C in Row 9. Pick up 10B and stitch through the fourth C away from where your thread is emerging in Row 9. Pick up 2B and stitch through the next C in Row 9. Pick up 12B and stitch through the fifth C away in Row 9. Stitch through the next 5C and the 4F at the bottom of the petal **(Fig. 6)**. Leave your working thread hanging for attaching the petals together. Weave in, secure, and trim your tail thread.

Note: The distance between the B added in step 10 should be slightly shorter than the distance between the C in the previous row. This allows you to push them gently behind the beads in Row 9 and creates the illusion of a smooth petal edge. Depending on the manufacturer of the beads that you use, you may need to add or subtract a few beads to each group in this step to achieve that effect.

11. Repeat steps 1–10 to create two more Large Petals.

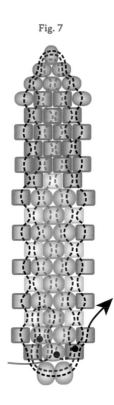

Fig. 7

Make the Large Side Petals

12. Needle up one yard of nylon thread and pick up 10F, 1E, 1C, 1D, 3C, and 4B. Stitch back through the first B added, creating a picot that will form the tip of the petal. Leave the tail thread just long enough to weave into the beadwork later and trim. For row 1, work three peyote stitches using 1C for each stitch and five more peyote stitches using 1F for each stitch **(Fig. 7, blue thread)**.

13. For Row 2, you will work in the direction back toward the tip of the petal. Work one peyote stitch with 1C, four peyote stitches using 1E for each stitch, one peyote stitch with 1D, two peyote stitches using 1C for each stitch, and one peyote stitch with 1B. Pass through all 3B of the picot. Working toward the petal bottom, work one peyote stitch with 1B, two peyote stitches using 1C for each stitch, one peyote stitch with 1D, and four peyote stitches using 1E for each stitch **(Fig. 7, red thread)**. Add one final C using an odd-count peyote stitch thread path to return to the C that you just added, heading away from the tip of the petal. Pick up 2F and stitch through the C on the other side of the petal to step up **(Fig. 7, brown thread)**.

14. For Row 3, work one peyote stitch with 1C, three peyote stitches using 1D for each stitch, three peyote stitches using 1C for each stitch, and one peyote stitch with 1B. Pass through all 5B at the tip of the petal. Work one peyote stitch with 1B, work three peyote stitches using 1C for each stitch, three peyote stitches using 1D for each stitch, and one peyote stitch with 1C. Stitch through the 2F at the bottom of the petal, then step up through to the first C added in this row **(Fig. 7, black thread)**.

15. For Row 4, work six peyote stitches using 1C for each stitch and one peyote stitch with 1B. Pass through all 7B on the tip of the petal. Work one peyote stitch using 1B and six peyote stitches using 1C for each stitch, then stitch through the next C, the 2F at the bottom of the petal, and the next 3C to step up **(Fig. 8, blue thread)**.

16. For Row 5, work five peyote stitches using 1C for each stitch and one peyote stitch with 1B. Pass through all 9B at the tip of the petal. Work one peyote stitch with 1B and five peyote stitches using 1C for each stitch. Stitch through the next 2C, the 2F at the bottom of the petal, and the next 6C to step up through the second C added in the previous row **(Fig. 8, red thread)**.

Note: If you cannot pass through the B at the tip of the petal because it is too full of thread, weave your thread through C instead until you reach the B where your thread would have emerged if you were able to pass through all 9B in a continuous manner.

17. For Row 6, work three peyote stitches using 1C for each stitch and one peyote stitch with 1B. Pass through all 11B in the tip of the petal, or weave through the C until your thread emerges from the 11th B. Working toward the bottom of the petal, work one peyote stitch with 1B and three peyote stitches using 1C for each stitch. Stitch through the next 2C **(Fig. 8, black thread)**.

18. For Row 7, reverse direction so that you are working the direction toward the tip of the petal. Stitch through the adjacent D and the next 3C. Work two peyote stitches using 1C for each stitch. Stitch through the next 2C. Make a U-turn in the beadwork by stitching through the adjacent B and the last 2C that you just passed. Bring your thread back out the last C added. Make a peyote stitch with 1B. Stitch through the next 3C and D. Reverse direction and stitch through the adjacent C **(Fig. 9, green thread)**.

19. To make one side edge of the petal, pick up 10B and stitch through the 13B along the tip, or weave through the C to bring your thread out of the last B on the other side of the petal **(Fig. 9, black thread)**.

20. For the other side edge of the petal, stitch through the next 2C. Work two peyote stitches using 1C for each stitch. Stitch through the next 3C. Make a U-turn in the beadwork by stitching through the adjacent C and the last 3C you just passed. Bring your thread back out of the last C added in this row. Work a peyote stitch with 1B. Stitch through the next 3C, then reverse direction and stitch through the adjacent B **(Fig. 9, red thread)**. Pick up 10B and stitch through the fourth C from the bottom of the petal. The shape of the petal should be symmetrical. Finish by stitching through the next 3C and the bottom 2F **(Fig. 9, blue thread)**. Leave your working thread hanging for attaching the other petals. Weave in, secure, and trim your tail thread.

21. Repeat steps 12–20 to create five more Large Side Petals.

Make the Small Side Petals

22. To start the Small Side Petal, follow steps 12–14.

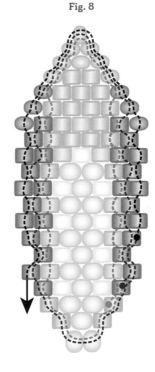

Fig. 8

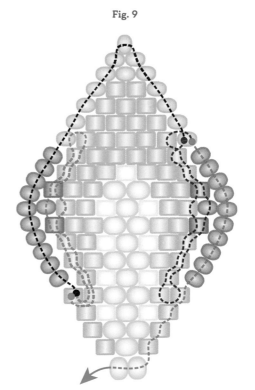

Fig. 9

23. Work six peyote stitches using 1C for each stitch and one peyote stitch using 1B. Pass through the 7B at the petal tip. Work one peyote stitch using 1B and six peyote stitches using 1C for each stitch. Stitch through the next C and 2F on the bottom of the petal, then through the next 3C to step up **(Fig. 10, black thread)**.

24. To make one side edge of the petal, stitch through the next D and C. Work three peyote stitches using 1B for each stitch. Stitch through the next 4C, then reverse direction and stitch through the adjacent B. Pick up 13B (making adjustments in the quantity of Bs, if necessary, to make the edge of the petal smooth) and stitch through the third C from the bottom, the next 2C and 2F on the bottom, and the next 3C on the other side of the petal **(Fig. 10, red thread)**.

25. For the other side edge, stitch through the next D and C. Work three peyote stitches using 1B for each stitch. Stitch through the next 4C, then reverse direction and stitch through the adjacent B. Pick up 13B (or the same number of beads that you used for the other side). Stitch through the third C from the bottom, then the next 2C and 2F on the bottom of the petal **(Fig. 10, blue thread)**. Weave in, secure, and trim your tail and working threads.

26. Repeat steps 22–25 to create five more Small Side Petals.

Assemble the Flowers

27. You will assemble each flower using one Large Petal, two Large Side Petals, two Small Side Petals, and a crystal pendant for the bottom petal. Place the petals into the arrangement shown in **Figure 11**; the two Large Side Petals should be on the top and the two Small Side Petals should be on the bottom. Needle up the working thread left hanging on one of the Large Side Petals. It should be emerging from the 2F at the bottom; if the thread is headed toward the other Large Side Petal, flip the petal over. Stitch through the 2F on the bottom of the adjacent Small Side Petal. Pick up 1F and stitch through the 2F on the bottom of the next Small Side Petal and then through the 2F on the bottom of the next Large Side Petal. Pick up 1F and stitch through the 2F on the bottom of the first Large Side Petal. This completes a circular thread path. Tighten the beads and retrace the thread path at

Fig. 10

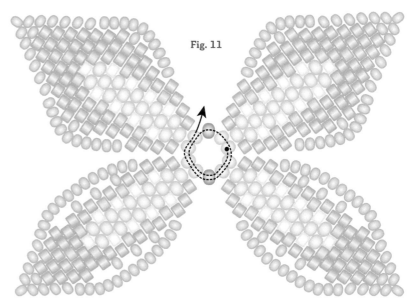

Fig. 11

least once for additional stability, then bring your thread out of the 2F on the bottom of the Large Side Petal next to the one from which you started **(Fig. 11)**.

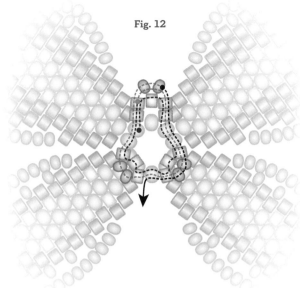

Fig. 12

28. Pick up 5E, skip the next F, and stitch through the 2F on the bottom of the next Large Side Petal. Pick up 3E, skip the 2F on the next Small Side Petal, and stitch through the F that you added in the last step. Pick up 3E, skip the 2F on the next Small Side Petal, and stitch through the 2F on the following Large Side Petal. Step up through the first 2E added **(Fig. 12, red thread)**.

29. Pick up 2A, skip the next E, and stitch through the next 2E, 2F, and E. Pick up 2A and skip the next E, stitch through the next E, the next F, and the next E. Pick up 2A, skip the next E, and stitch through the next E, 2F, and 2E, and step up through the first 2A added **(Fig. 12, blue thread)**. Stitch through the next 2E, 2F, E, 2A, E, and F. Your thread should be emerging from the bottom center F in the flower assembly **(Fig. 12, black thread)**. Leave your working thread hanging for attaching the pendant later.

30. Needle up the working thread that is emerging from the bottom 4F in the Central Petal. Turn the assembled side petals over to the back side. Lay the Central Petal on the assembled side petals so that the 4F on the bottom of the Central Petal are roughly centered. You will first attach the Central Petal to the Small Side Petals. Stitch through the bottommost single F in the nearest Small Side Petal. *Moving in the direction toward the petal's tip, pass through the next F. Reverse direction to stitch through the adjacent F. Stitch back through the single F of the Small Side Petal, then through the 4F on the bottom of the Central Petal. Stitch through the bottommost single F in the opposite Small Side Petal. Repeat from * once to join the other Small Side Petal **(Fig. 13)**.

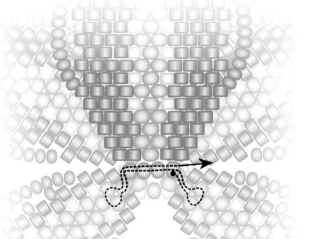

Fig. 13

31. Attach the Central Petal to the Large Side Petals. Stitch through the nearest C on the bottom edge of the Central Petal. Then stitch through the nearest F in the Large Side Petal; this F should be the second one from the bottom, near the right edge. Stitch through the next E, then reverse direction and stitch through the adjacent F. Stitch back through the first F that you passed on the side petal and the C in the Central Petal. Stitch through the 4F on the bottom of the Central Petal. Repeat from the beginning of the step to join the other Large Side Petal **(Fig. 14, black thread)**. Stitch back through the nearest C on the bottom edge the Central Petal, the nearest F in the Large Side Petal, the next E, and the next F. Reverse direction and stitch through the adjacent F **(Fig. 14, blue thread)**.

32. You'll work on the back side of the assembled petals to add extra beadwork to stiffen the assembly and stitch to the stem later. Pick up 5F and stitch down through the F second from the bottom of the Central Petal, then up through the adjacent F. For these 2F and any subsequent pair that you stitch through, work towards the bottom when you are passing through the first F and reverse direction when passing through the second F. Pick up 5F and stitch through the pair of F second from the bottom of the next Large Side Petal. Pick up 4F and stitch through the pair of F second from the bottom of the nearby Small Side Petal. Pick up 6F and stitch through the pair of F in the second from the bottom of the next Small Side Petal. Pick up 4F and stitch through the nearest F of the next Large Side Petal, next to the one where you started **(Fig. 15)**. Retrace the thread path at least twice to reinforce the connection. If you have at least 12 inches (30.5 cm) of thread, you can leave it hanging to use later. Weave

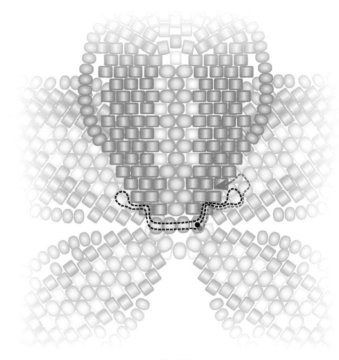

Fig. 14

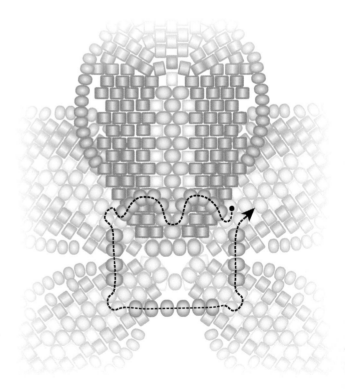

Fig. 15

in, secure, and trim any other additional working threads, except for the one that you left hanging from the F on the bottom of the assembled petals in step 29.

33. Turn the assembled petals over to the front to attach the bottom petal. Needle up the thread hanging from the bottom F. Pick up 13A and one pear-shaped pendant. Stitch through the same F into the same side of the bead from which you exited **(Fig. 16)**.

34. Pick up 5A. Skip the first 5A in the group of 13A and stitch through the next 3A and the pendant, moving from the front of the necklace to the back **(Fig. 17)**.

35. Pick up 5A and stitch back through the F on the bottom of the assembled petals on the same side you last exited. Stitch through the first 5A in the first group of 13A added in step 33. Make sure the new group of 5A sits behind the group of 5A added in the previous step and the pendant **(Fig. 18)**.

Fig. 16

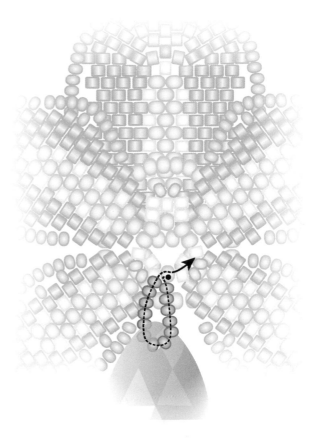

Fig. 17

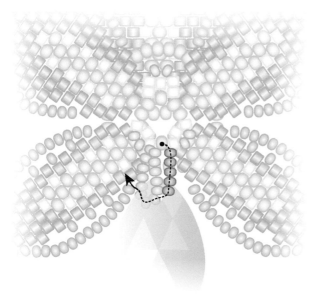

Fig. 18

36. Pick up 1A. Stitch through the adjacent group of 5A on the front side of the pendant, then the F at the bottom of the petal assembly **(Fig. 19)**. Weave in, secure, and trim the thread.

37. Repeat steps 27–36 to create two more flowers.

Make the Stem

38. Needle up about 48 inches (1.2 m) of braided fishing line thread. Make the first half of the stem segment. Pick up 34F and leave just enough of a tail to weave into the beadwork later and trim on the first segment. With medium tension, stitch 12 rows of flat even-count peyote stitch using 1F for each stitch for a total of 14 rows.

39. Zip the peyote strip into a tube. Stitch through the nearest bead on the opposite row, then pass through the next bead on the first row **(Fig. 20)**. Continue stitching until you reach the other end of the strip. Make sure to pass through the first F in the first row to bring the beads completely together. Weave in, secure, and trim the tail thread. Leave the working thread hanging.

40. Repeat steps 38 and 39 to make the second half of the stem segment, leaving about 14 inches (35.6 cm) of tail thread.

Fig. 19

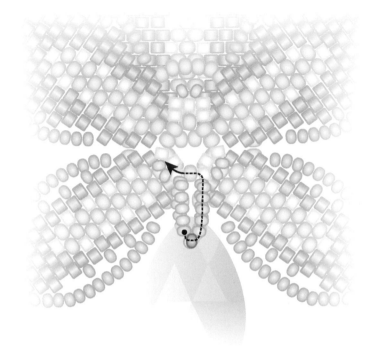

Fig. 20

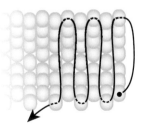

41. Make a partially zipped stem segment. Follow step 38 to create a peyote strip. Start zipping the peyote strip into a tube; stop when you've zipped 20 beads together. The last seven beads on each edge should be left unzipped and will form a leaf.

42. Weave through the F along the unzipped edge of the peyote strip. When you're halfway up the first unzipped edge, start stitching through the F in a diagonal direction until you bring the thread out of the F at the center of the strip's open edge **(Fig. 21, blue thread)**.

43. Pick up 7F then stitch back through the fourth to the last F. Work a peyote stitch with 1F, then pick up 1F and stitch back through the middle F along the leaf edge. Reverse direction and stitch through the adjacent F and the last F added in this step **(Fig. 21, black thread)**.

44. Work two peyote stitches using 1F for each stitch. Pass through all 3F at the tip of the stem segment, then work two more peyote stitches using 1F for each stitch. Stitch through the middle F on the edge of the original peyote strip, then through the adjacent F **(Fig. 22, red thread)**. Repeat from the beginning of the step, but after finishing the last peyote stitch, pass through the third F from the left edge of the peyote strip. Reverse direction and stitch through the adjacent F, which is two beads from the left edge, and the last F added in this step **(Fig. 22, black thread)**.

45. Work one peyote stitch with 1F. Pass through all 7F at the tip. Work another peyote stitch using 1F, then stitch through the second F from the right edge of the original peyote strip. Reverse direction and stitch through the adjacent F, which is the last one on the edge **(Fig. 23, red thread)**. Repeat from the beginning of the step, passing through all 9F on the tip. After finishing the last peyote stitch, pass through the second bead from the left edge, then reverse direction and stitch through the adjacent F and the F just added **(Fig. 23, black thread)**. Weave in, secure, and trim your thread.

46. Repeat steps 41–45 to make another partially zipped stem segment.

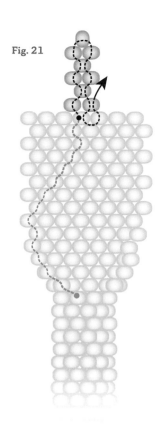

Fig. 21

Fig. 22

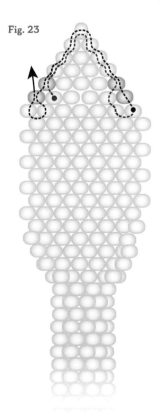

Fig. 23

Make the Chain

Fig. 24

47. You will make one link of the chain at a time with right-angle weave. Needle up a wingspan of braided fishing line thread and pick up 20A. Stitch through the first 12 again to form a loop and bring your working thread opposite the tail thread. Leave at least 12 inches (30.5 cm) of tail thread to join the stem later.

48. Pick up 18A. Stitch through the center 2A in the last loop formed, then stitch through the first 10A added in the new loop **(Fig. 24)**.

49. Repeat step 48 ten more times for a total of 12 loops. You can make more or fewer loops depending on your desired necklace length. Each loop will add approximately ¾ inch (2 cm).

50. The last three loops will hold your toggle clasp so you have sizing options for your necklace. You can insert either side of the double button into any of the three loops on the end of the necklace for six different positions and lengths. Pick up 34A. Stitch through the middle 2A in the last loop, then the first 18A added. Repeat this step twice to add two more loops.

Fig. 25

51. Pick up 3F and stitch through the middle two A in the loop **(Fig. 25)**. Weave down through all the loops in the chain. Weave in, secure, and trim the tail thread. Leave the working thread hanging to attach to the stem later.

52. Repeat steps 47–51 to make the second half of the chain.

Assembly

53. Attach the two completely zipped stem segments. Position the stem segments so the beads at the two ends are lined up. Using the tail thread hanging on one segment, pick up 2F and stitch into the corresponding F on the opposite stem segment. Reverse direction and exit through the adjacent F

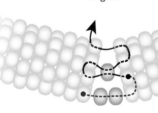

Fig. 26

(Fig. 26, pink thread). Pick up 1F, and stitch through the corresponding F on the first stem segment. Reverse direction and exit through the adjacent F. Stitch back through the new F and into the next F on the end of the second stem segment. Reverse direction and stitch through the adjacent F. Without adding any beads, stitch through the aligned F on the first stem segment **(Fig. 26, black thread)**.

54. Turn the beadwork over to attach the other side of the segment. Reverse direction and stitch through the adjacent F. Pick up 1F and stitch through the corresponding F on the opposite stem segment. Reverse direction and stitch out through the adjacent F. Stitch back through the new F and into the next F on the end of the first stem segment.

Retrace the thread path connecting the stem segments at least once until the combined stem is firm and doesn't bend. If you have more than one working thread in this spot, weave in, secure, and trim the shorter thread, leaving the other for attaching to the middle orchid.

Fig. 27

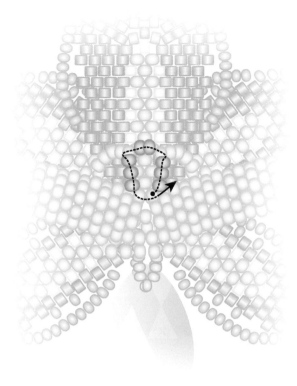

55. Repeat steps 53 and 54 to attach one partially zipped stem segment to each end of the combined stem, being mindful of the orientation of the leaf ends. Try to position the partially zipped segments so that the leaves will lie flat when the necklace lies flat. Leave one thread hanging from each of the three joins in the stem to attach the flowers.

56. To begin attaching a flower, bring one of the working threads out of the F at a stem join, above the zipped section of the stem, moving away from the zipped section. Turn both the flower and stem over; the leaves of the stem should be facing down. You'll attach the flower from the back. Pick up 3F. Working toward the center of the flower, stitch through the last F in the group of 5F on the back of the Central Petal. Pick up 2F and stitch through the first F in the next group of 5F on the Central Petal. Pick up 4F and stitch through the F in the stem that is aligned with the F from which you started. Then stitch through that starting F again **(Fig. 27)**. Retrace the thread path at least once to reinforce. Weave in, secure, and trim the thread.

Fig. 28

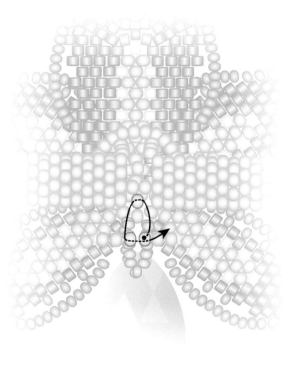

57. Using the working thread on the back side of the flower, bring it out of the fourth F in the bottom group of 6F that joins the two Small Side Petals together. Stitch through the single F added between the stems near the bottom of the stem join, on the front side of the join. Stitch through the third and fourth F in the group of 6F between the two Small Side Petals **(Fig. 28)**. The three beads included in

this thread path are outlined in black in Fig. 31. Retrace the thread path at least once to reinforce. Weave in, secure, and trim the thread.

58. Attach the chain to the partially zipped stem segment by inserting the first loop of the chain into the end of the tube. The loop will not fully fit in the tube and will just sit on the outside. Needle up the hanging thread on the chain and stitch through two or three F on the end of the tube, then back through the first couple A in the chain **(Fig. 29)**. Retrace the thread path at least twice to securely fasten the chain to the stem segment. Repeat to attach the other chain to the partially zipped stem segment at the opposite end of the stem.

Make the Toggle

59. You will make three flower buds to create the toggle. Needle up one yard (91.4 cm) of braided fishing line thread and pick up 8F. Stitch through the first F again to form a loop, leaving a 12-inch (30.5 cm) tail **(Fig. 30, blue thread)**. If desired, stitch through all the beads once more.

60. Pick up 3F, skip the next F in the loop, and stitch through the following F. Repeat three times, then step up through the first 2F added **(Fig. 30, red thread)**.

61. Pick up 2F and stitch through the middle F in the next group of 3F in the previous round. Repeat three times, then step up through the first pair of F added **(Fig. 30, black thread)**.

62. Pick up 1F and stitch through the next pair of F in the previous round. Repeat three times, then step up through the first F added **(Fig. 31, red thread)**.

63. Pick up 2E and stitch through the next F in the previous round. Repeat three times, then step up through the first pair of E added **(Fig. 31, black thread)**.

Fig. 29

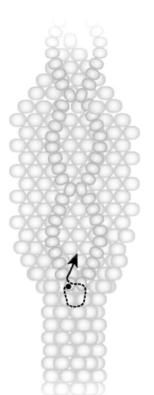

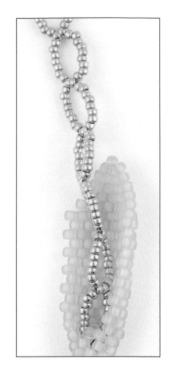

Fig. 30

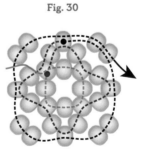

Fig. 31

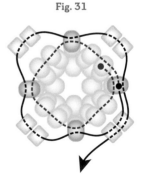

64. Pick up 1E and stitch through the next 2E in the previous row. Repeat three times, then step up through the first E added **(Fig. 32, blue thread)**.

65. Pick up 1E and stitch through the next E in the previous row. Repeat three times, then step up through the first E added **(Fig. 32, red thread)**.

66. Pick up 1A and stitch through the next E in the previous row. Repeat three times **(Fig. 32, black thread)**. Weave in, secure, and trim your working thread.

67. Needle up the tail thread. Pick up 2F, skip the next F, and stitch through the following F. Repeat three times. Do not step up; instead stitch through the next F toward the center of the bud **(Fig. 33)**.

68. Repeat steps 59–67 to create a total of three buds. Leave your needle on the working thread hanging from your last completed bud.

69. To join the buds, pick up 5F and stitch through 3F on the bottom of another toggle bud **(Fig. 34, pink thread)**. Pick up 1F, skip the last F in the group of 5F added, then stitch through the next 2F. Pick up 2F and stitch through 3F in the bottom of the remaining toggle bud **(Fig. 34, blue thread)**. Pick up 1F, skip the last F in the last group of 2F added, and stitch through the first F. Stitch through the center F in the first group of 5F added, then pass through the next F back toward the first bud. Pick up 1F and stitch through the F at the bottom of the first bud, across from the F from which you started, and the next F **(Fig. 34)**. Retrace the thread path at least once to reinforce. Weave in, secure, and trim the thread.

Fig. 32

Fig. 33

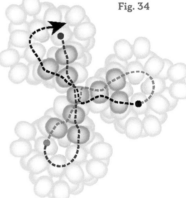

Fig. 34

Snail Shell Necklace

The spiraling shell of terrestrial snails and other mollusks is a fascinating example of mathematical patterns found in nature. This amazing shape forms thanks to a biochemical process that allows the shell to form from the center and grow outward as the snail becomes larger. This necklace spotlights the gorgeous coiling shape that is one of the miracles of the natural world.

TECHNIQUES

Cubic right-angle weave (CRAW)
(page 11)

Peyote stitch (page 5)

INSTRUCTIONS

Make Snail A

1. Needle up a wingspan of thread and pick up 4A. Leave the thread tail just long enough to weave into the beadwork later. Create the first CRAW unit; pick up [1B, 1A, 1B] to make the first side, [1B, 1A] for both the second and third sides, and 1A for the fourth side. The top and bottom of the unit consists of A beads (**Fig. 1**). Make sure to step up after completing this unit and all the others that follow.

Symbols

- A
- B
- C
- D
- E
- F
- 2-mm pearl
- 3-mm pearl
- 4-mm pearl
- 3-mm bicone
- 4-mm bicone

Fig. 1

Snail A
Unit 1

Side 1   Side 2   Side 3   Side 4

SKILL LEVEL

Intermediate

DIMENSIONS

5 inches (12.7 cm) wide and 17 inches (43.18 cm) long

MATERIALS

5 g matte light bronze size 15º seed beads (A)

5 g stable finish galvanized champagne gold size 15º seed beads (B)

1 g ceylon ivory size 15º seed beads (C)

10 g matte light bronze size 11º seed beads (D)

6 g stable finish galvanized champagne gold size 11º seed beads (E)

2 g ceylon ivory size 11º seed beads (F)

134 cerulean blue glass pearls, 2 mm

166 iridescent light blue crystal pearls, 3 mm

75 iridescent light blue crystal pearls, 4 mm

160 crystal bicones AB, 3 mm

15 crystal bicones AB, 4 mm

Crystal braided fishing line thread, 6 lb

TOOLS

Beader's Tool Kit (page 2)

Size 12 beading needles

2. You will gradually increase the size of each subsequent CRAW unit by using different combinations of size 11° seed beads to make the sides of each unit. For Units 2–5, pick up [1E, 1A, 1B] to make Side 1 of each unit; [1B, 1A] to make Sides 2 and 3; and 1A to make Side 4 **(Fig. 2)**.

3. For Unit 6, pick up [1E, 1D, 1E] for Side 1; [1B, 1A] for Sides 2 and 3; and 1A for side 4 **(Fig. 3)**.

4. For Units 7–22, pick up [1E, 1D, 1E] for Side 1; [1E, 1D] for Side 2; [1B, 1D] for Side 3; and 1D for Side 4 **(Fig. 4)**.

5. For Unit 23, pick up [1E, 1D, 1E] for Side 1; [1E, 1D] for Sides 2 and 3; and 1D for Side 4 **(Fig. 5)**.

6. For Units 24 and 25, pick up [1E, 2D, 1E] for Side 1; [1E, 2D] for Sides 2 and 3; and 2D for Side 4 **(Fig. 6)**. The 25th unit will form the opening of the snail shell.

7. After finishing Unit 25 and stepping up, you will make three embellishment columns that run the entire length of the CRAW tube. Stitch down through the very next E (the first one you added in the last unit). This should position your thread along the column of beads in the CRAW rope that has the largest seed beads **(Fig. 7, pink thread)**.

8. Pick up one 2-mm pearl and stitch through the next E down the CRAW tube to peyote stitch the bead in place **(Fig. 7, black thread)**. Repeat six times for a total of seven peyote-stitched 2-mm pearls. Make 12 more peyote stitches using one 3-mm pearl for each and six more peyote stitches using one 2-mm pearl for each.

9. After adding the last 2-mm pearl, stitch through the next 2A on the end of the CRAW tube, then down through the next B in the same unit. This should position your thread along the column opposite of the one where you added the pearls **(Fig. 8)**.

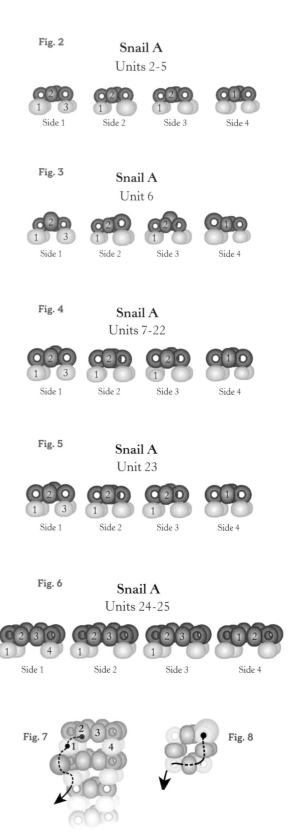

Fig. 2

Snail A
Units 2-5

Side 1   Side 2   Side 3   Side 4

Fig. 3

Snail A
Unit 6

Side 1   Side 2   Side 3   Side 4

Fig. 4

Snail A
Units 7-22

Side 1   Side 2   Side 3   Side 4

Fig. 5

Snail A
Unit 23

Side 1   Side 2   Side 3   Side 4

Fig. 6

Snail A
Units 24-25

Side 1   Side 2   Side 3   Side 4

Fig. 7   Fig. 8

10. You will now create the second embellishment column. Stitch through the next 8B; pull tightly to cause your CRAW tube to curl more. Make six peyote stitches using 1C for each and 10 peyote stitches using 1F for each.

11. When you reach the end of the CRAW tube, stitch through the 2D to the right of the E from which your thread is emerging. Stitch down through the next E to head back down the CRAW tube **(Fig. 9)**.

Fig. 9

12. You will now create the third embellishment column, which is visible on the front side of the necklace. Begin by making 18 peyote stitches using 1F for each and six peyote stitches using 1C for each.

Fig. 10

13. Pick up three repeats of [1C, 1B]. Stitch through the last C added to the CRAW tube using peyote stitch and the next B to form a circle. Stitch through the first C, B, and C added **(Fig. 10)**.

14. Pick up 5A and stitch through the second to last C added to the CRAW tube using peyote stitch, the next B, the last C added in peyote stitch, and the next B **(Fig. 11)**.

Fig. 11

15. Reinforce the thread path from steps 13 and 14, then weave in, secure, and trim the thread.

16. To finish the snail opening, start a new 24-inch (61 cm) length of thread near the opening and bring it out of the 25th CRAW unit, through the last E in the first embellishment column, with the 2-mm pearl attached. Stitch through the next 2D. Pick up 1E and stitch through the next 2D. Pick up 2F and stitch through the next 2D. Pick up 1E and stitch through the next 2D. Pick up one 2-mm pearl and stitch through the next 2D **(Fig. 12, pink thread)**. Stitch through the next E, 2D, and 1F **(Fig. 12, black thread)**. If your snail shell isn't spiraling in on itself already, gently coax it into a spiral shape, placing the beginning of the CRAW rope at the center.

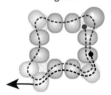

Fig. 12

17. Pick up 1F and stitch through the E between the 11th and 12th 3-mm pearls in the first embellishment column. Stitch back through the F just added and the next F in the snail opening **(Fig. 13, pink thread)**. Stitch through the remaining beads on the end of the CRAW tube **(Fig. 13, black thread)**. Reinforce the thread path again.

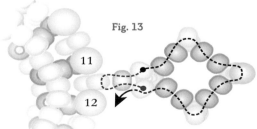

Fig. 13

11

12

18. You will add five pieces of fringe to the end of the CRAW tube. Stitch through the next F, 2D, and E in the 25th CRAW unit, away from the open end of the snail. Stitch through the next D in the same CRAW unit. Your thread should be emerging between 2D in the second to last CRAW unit, on the front side of the snail. Bring your thread to the inside of the snail shell opening **(Fig. 14)**.

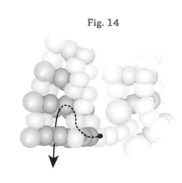

Fig. 14

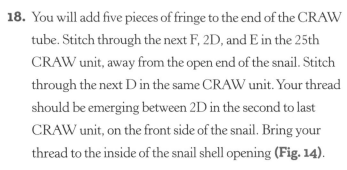

Fig. 15

19. Your thread should be located in the D marked with a blue 1 in **Figure 15**. To start Fringe 1: pick up 3A, 1B, 14 repeats of [one 3-mm bicone, 1B], one 4-mm bicone, 1E, and 1B. Skip the last B and stitch back through the rest of the beads added, then through the next 2D in the second to last CRAW unit **(Fig. 15)**. Your thread should emerge from the D marked with a blue 2.

20. For Fringe 2, repeat step 19, but use only 13 repeats of [one 3-mm bicone, 1B]. At the end of this step, your thread should emerge from the D marked with a blue 3 in **Figure 15**.

21. For Fringe 3, repeat step 19, but use only 12 repeats of the [one 3 mm bicone, B] and stitch through only 1D in the second to last CRAW unit. At the end of this step, your thread should emerge from the D marked with a blue 4 in **Figure 15**.

22. For Fringe 4, repeat step 19, but use 15 repeats of [one 3-mm bicone, 1B] and stitch through only 1D in the second to last CRAW unit. At the end of this step, your thread should emerge from the D marked with a blue 5 in **Figure 15**.

23. For Fringe 5, repeat step 19, but use 16 repeats of [one 3-mm bicone, 1B].

24. If necessary, weave through the CRAW tube toward the end of the spiral to sew a stitch or two of your choice between the two overlapping parts of the snail to hold the spiral snail shape in place. Then weave in, secure, and trim the thread.

Make Snail B

25. Repeat steps 1–4 to create the first 19 CRAW units.

26. For Unit 20, repeat step 5.

27. For Units 21–22, repeat step 6.

28. To create the first embellishment column, follow steps 7–9, but use the following beads for the peyote stitches: nine 2-mm pearls, seven 3-mm pearls, and six 2-mm pearls (one pearl for each stitch).

29. To create the second embellishment column, follow steps 10–11, but after stitching through the first 8E, use the following beads for the peyote stitches: 7C and 6F (one bead for each stitch).

30. To create the third embellishment column, follow the instructions outlined in steps 12–15 but use the following beads for the peyote stitches: 15F and 6C (one bead for each stitch).

31. Finish the opening of Snail B by repeating steps 16–18.

32. You will make four pieces of fringe for Snail B. Follow steps 19–22, but use the following beads: 12 repeats of [one 3-mm bicone, 1B] for Fringe 1, 11 repeats of [one 3-mm bicone, 1B] for Fringe 2, 10 repeats of [one 3-mm bicone, 1B] for Fringe 3, and 13 repeats of the [one 3-mm bicone, 1B] for Fringe 4, in addition to the one 4-mm bicone, 1E, and 1B at the end of each fringe. Make sure the longest fringe is placed on the side of the snail opening with the 2-mm pearl. Follow step 24 if necessary.

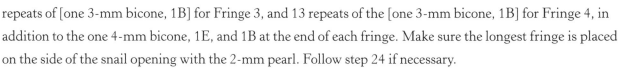

Make Snail C

33. Repeat steps 1–4 to create the first 16 CRAW units.

34. For Unit 17, repeat step 5.

35. For Units 18–19, repeat step 6.

36. To create the first embellishment column, follow steps 7–9, but use the following beads for the peyote stitches: seven 2-mm pearls, five 3-mm pearls, six 2-mm pearls (one pearl for each stitch).

37. To create the second embellishment column, follow steps 10–11, but after stitching through the first 8E, use the following beads for the peyote stitches: 6C and 4F (one bead for each stitch).

38. To create the third embellishment column, follow steps 12–15, but use the following beads for the peyote stitches: 13F and 5C (one for each stitch).

39. Finish the opening of Snail B by repeating steps 16–18.

40. You will make three pieces of fringe for Snail C. Follow steps 19–21, but use the following beads: eight repeats of [one 3-mm bicone, 1B] for Fringe 1, nine repeats of [one 3-mm bicone, 1B] for Fringe 2, and 10 repeats of [one 3-mm bicone, 1B] for Fringe 3, in addition to the one 4-mm bicone, 1E, and 1B at the end of each fringe. Make sure the longest fringe is placed on the side of the snail opening with the 2-mm pearl. Follow step 24 if necessary.

Make Snail D

41. Repeat steps 1–4 to create the first 13 CRAW units.

42. For Unit 14, repeat step 5.

43. For Units 15–16, repeat step 6.

44. To create the first embellishment column, follow steps 7–9, but use the following beads for the peyote stitches: six 2-mm pearls, four 3-mm pearls, and five 2-mm pearls (one for each stitch).

45. To create the second embellishment column, follow steps 10–11, but after stitching through the first 8E, use the following beads for the peyote stitches: 6C and 1F (one for each stitch).

46. To create the third embellishment column, follow steps 12–15, but for the peyote stitches, use the following beads: 10F and 5C (one for each stitch).

47. Finish the opening of Snail B by repeating steps 16–18.

48. You will make three pieces of fringe for Snail D. Follow steps 19–21, but use the following beads: five repeats of [one 3-mm bicone, 1B] for Fringe 1, six repeats of [one 3-mm bicone, 1B] for Fringe 2, and seven repeats of [one 3-mm bicone, 1B] for Fringe 3, in addition to the one 4-mm bicone, 1E, and 1B at the end of each fringe. Make sure the longest fringe is placed on the side of the snail opening with the 2-mm pearl. Follow step 24 if necessary.

Make Snail E

49. Repeat steps 1–2 to create the first five CRAW units.

50. For Unit 6, repeat step 3.

51. For Units 7–11, repeat step 4.

52. For Unit 12, repeat step 5.

53. For Unit 13, repeat step 6.

54. To create the first embellishment column, follow steps 7–9, but use the following beads for the peyote stitches: four 2-mm pearls, three 3-mm pearls, and five 2-mm pearls (one pearl for each stitch).

55. To create the second embellishment column, follow steps 10–11, but after stitching through the first 8E, use the following beads for the peyote stitches: 3C and 1F (one bead for each stitch).

56. To create the second embellishment column, follow steps 12–15, but for the peyote stitches, use the following beads: 7F and 5C (one for each stitch). There is no fringe on Snail E. Finish the opening by repeating steps 16–18. Weave in, secure, and trim your thread.

57. Repeat steps 49–56 seven more times for a total of eight Snail Es to create a 17-inch (43.2 cm) necklace. Create additional Snail Es for more length. Each additional Snail E will add approximately ¾ inch (1.9 cm).

Assembly

58. To attach Snail A to Snail B, secure a new 12-inch (30.5 cm) length of thread close to the attachment point on Snail A. Bring your thread out of the seventh 3-mm pearl on the outside of Snail A, counting from the fringe end to the inside of the spiral. Pick up 1D and stitch into the fourth 2-mm pearl, counting from the fringe end.

Pick up 1D and stitch through the 3-mm pearl on Snail A again to form a RAW unit to attach the two snails together **(Fig. 16)**. Retrace the thread path at least twice to reinforce, then weave in, secure, and trim the thread.

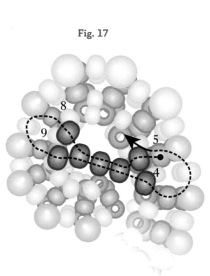

Fig. 16

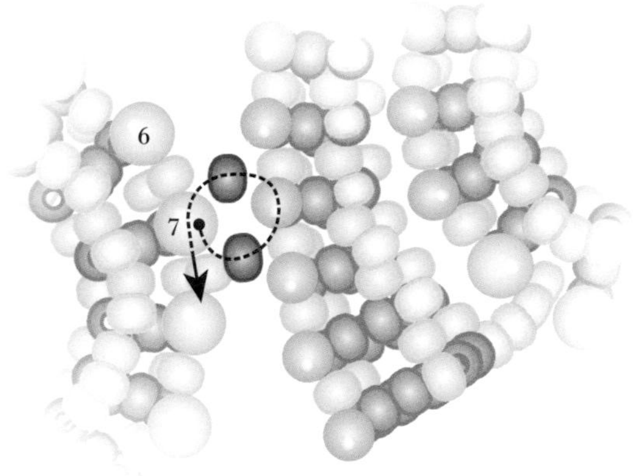

Snail A   Snail B

59. To attach Snail B to Snail C, secure a new 12-inch (30.5 cm) length of thread close to the attachment point on Snail B. Repeat step 58 to complete the attachment, but bring your thread out of the fourth 3-mm pearl on the outside of Snail B, counting from the fringe end to the inside of the spiral.

60. To attach Snail C to Snail D, secure a new 12-inch (30.5 cm) length of thread close to the attachment point on Snail C. Repeat step 58 to complete the attachment, but bring your thread out of the fourth 3-mm pearl on the outside of Snail C, counting from the fringe end to the inside of the spiral. Use the third 2-mm pearl as the other attachment point.

61. To attach Snail D to Snail E, secure a new 12-inch (30.5 cm) length of thread close to the attachment point on Snail D. Repeat step 60 to join the two components.

62. To attach one Snail E to another Snail E, secure a new 12-inch (30.5 cm) length of thread close to the attachment point on one of the components. Repeat step 58 to complete the attachment, but bring your thread out of the first 2-mm pearl after the third 3-mm pearl on the first Snail E (counting from the open end of the CRAW tube) and use the third 2-mm pearl as the other attachment point. Repeat this step to connect all but one of the remaining Snail E components.

63. The remaining Snail E will be used as a button for the necklace clasp. Start a new 12-inch (30.5 cm) length of thread and bring it out on the back side of Snail E through the D between the fourth and fifth CRAW units from the open end of the CRAW tube. Your thread should be headed toward the center of the snail. Pick up 5D and stitch through the A between the eighth and ninth CRAW units from the open end, then stitch through the next E in the ninth unit and the next A. Pick up 1D and stitch back through the middle 3D in the group of 5D just added. Pick up 1D and stitch through the D between the third and fourth CRAW units from the open end, then the next E and D in the fourth unit to complete the thread path **(Fig. 17)**. Retrace the thread path at least twice to reinforce, then weave in, secure, and trim your thread.

Fig. 17

64. Start a new 18-inch length (45.7 cm) of thread in the last Snail E on the necklace and bring it out of the first 2-mm pearl after the third 3-mm pearl from the open end of the snail. To connect the Snail E button to the other snail components, pick up 11A and stitch through the middle D in the group of 5D added to the back of the button in the last step. Pick up another 11A and stitch through the first 2-mm pearl after the third 2-mm pearl in the last Snail E on the necklace **(Fig. 18)**. Retrace the thread path at least twice to reinforce, then weave in, secure, and trim your thread.

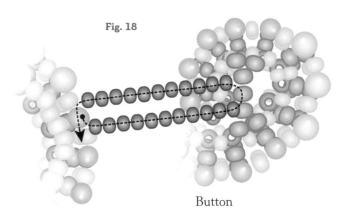

Fig. 18

Button

Snail E

Create the Pearl Strands

65. Needle up a new wingspan of thread and secure it in Snail A. To make Pearl Strand A, bring it out of the third 3-mm pearl peyote stitched to the outside from the fringe end, moving toward that end. Pick up 3A, 1D, then 46 repeats of [one 3-mm pearl, 1B]. Pick up 1E, then 11 repeats of [one 3-mm pearl, 1B] for the button loop. Skip the last 11 bead pairs; stitch back through the next E, the rest of the bead pairs, and the following D. Pick up 3A and stitch through the same 3-mm pearl on the outside of the snail. To prepare to make the next pearl strand, stitch through the next E and the next 3-mm pearl, moving toward the fringe end.

66. To make Pearl Strand B, pick up 3A, 1D, and 37 repeats of [one 4-mm pearl, 1B]. Pick up one more B and stitch through the E at the start of the button loop, the button loop, and the same E again. Stitch back through all the bead pairs and the following D. Pick up 2A and stitch through the third A in the adjacent group of 3A from Pearl Strand A, then the same 3-mm pearl at which you started. To prepare to make the next pearl strand, stitch through the next E and 3-mm pearl.

67. To make Pearl Strand C, pick up 3A, 1D, and 38 repeats of [one 4-mm pearl, 1B]. Pick up one more B and stitch through the E at the start of the button loop, the button loop, and the same E again. Stitch back through all bead pairs and the following D. Pick up 2A and stitch through the third A in the adjacent group of 3A from Pearl Strand B, then the same 3-mm pearl at which you started. To prepare to make the next pearl strand, stitch through the next E and the following 2-mm pearl.

68. To make Pearl Strand D, pick up 3A, 1D, and 49 repeats of [one 3-mm pearl, 1B]. Pick up one more B and stitch through the E at the start of the button loop, the button loop, and the same E again. Stitch back through all bead pairs and the following D. Pick up 2A and stitch through the third A in the adjacent group of 3A from Pearl Strand C, then the same 2-mm pearl at which you started. Weave in, secure, and trim your thread.

Tip: You can arrange your pearl strands straight or twisted around each other for different looks.

Moon Cycle Necklace

Having always lived in rural areas, I've spent a lot of time gazing at the full moon. Its blue light illuminates the natural landscape and is even bright enough for reading. On a clear night, it is almost too bright to look at directly. In this necklace, a combination of netting and peyote stitch capture stones that evoke the moon's shining light. The components decrease in size, depicting the shape of the moon as it waxes and wanes.

MATERIALS

4 g galvanized pewter size 15º seed beads (A)

1 g platinum-plated size 15º seed beads (B)

1 g matte gold-lined crystal size 15º seed beads (C)

3 g galvanized pewter size 11º seed beads (D)

3 g metallic steel iris size 10º cylinder beads (E)

1 g galvanized light pewter size 11º cylinder beads (F)

120 gray glass pearls, 2 mm

82 vintage gold crystal pearls, 3 mm

24 golden shadow crystal rounds, 4 mm

18 crystal/silver crystal rose montées, SS12/PP24

1 golden shadow Solaris crystal stone, 23 mm

6 golden shadow Solaris crystal stones, 14 mm

1 golden shadow crystal navette pendant, 30 mm

6 two-hole, open back natural brass settings for 14-mm Solaris stones

Oxidized brass-plated steel square wire oval cable chain, 7 inches (17.8 cm)

2 natural brass 15-gauge jump rings, 10 mm

1 natural brass hook closure, 20 × 7 mm

Braided fishing line thread, 6 lb.

SKILL LEVEL

Advanced

DIMENSIONS

16¹/2 inches (41.9 cm) long and 4 inches (10.2 cm) from top to bottom

TOOLS

Beader's Tool Kit (page 2)

Size 12 beading needles

2 pairs of chain- or flat-nose pliers

Wire cutters

TECHNIQUES

Netting (page 8)

Tubular peyote stitch (page 7)

Even-count peyote stitch (page 6)

Right-angle weave (RAW) (page 10)

Three-sided prismatic right-angle weave (PRAW-3) (page 12)

Note: The length of the necklace can be made longer with a longer length of chain.

Symbols

● A		●	2-mm pearl
○ B		●	3-mm pearl
● C		●	4-mm round
● D			
■ E		●	Rose montée
▪ F			

INSTRUCTIONS

Make the Full Moon Centerpiece

1. Needle up two wingspans of thread and pick up
   48E. Stitch through the first two beads again to
   form a loop, leaving a tail thread just long enough
   to weave into the beadwork later and trim. Work
   two rounds of peyote stitch, using 1E for each stitch
   and making sure to step up through the first bead
   added in each round after completing each round
   (Fig. 1).

2. You will now start the back side of the bezel for the
   23-mm stone. On the inside of the circle, make two
   rounds of peyote stitch, using 1D for each stitch
   and making sure to step up at the end of each round
   (Fig. 2).

3. Pick up 7A, skip the next D in the previous round,
   and stitch through the following D. Repeat 11 times,
   then step up through the first 4A added **(Fig. 3)**.

4. Pick up 2F and stitch through the middle A in the
   next group of 7A from the previous round. Repeat
   11 times then step up through the first 2F added
   (Fig. 4).

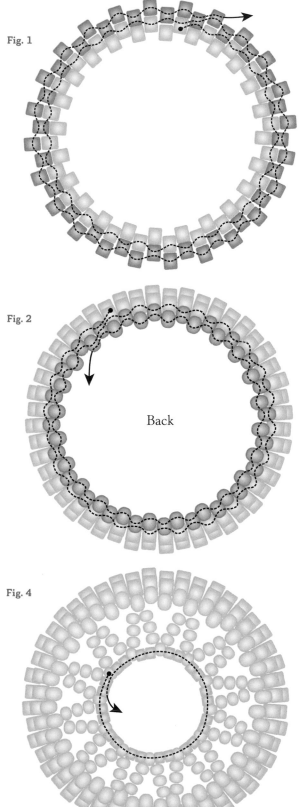

Fig. 1

Fig. 2

Back

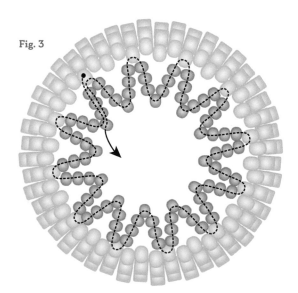

Fig. 3

Fig. 4

5. Pick up 1A and stitch through the next 2F. Repeat 11 times; do not step up. Stitch through the next 3A in the last group of seven, the next 2D, and the next 4E to the outer round of the bezel **(Fig. 5)**. The back of the bezel is complete.

6. Turn the beadwork over to the front. Place the 23-mm stone face up into the bezel and hold it in place as you work. Work one round of peyote stitch, using 1F for each stitch, and step up through the first F added **(Fig. 6)**. As you work, try to position your stone in the bezel so that there is an F directly on the lines that form the stone's facets.

7. Make two peyote stitches, using 1A for each stitch. These two A should sit between the lines that form the facets. If they do not, take them off and weave over an F and try again until they are in the correct position. Pick up one rose montée, slide it down your thread, and hold it face up against the 23-mm stone as you work. Pick up 3B. Stitch through the second hole in the rose montée, then the next F in the previous round **(Fig. 7, pink thread)**. Repeat from the beginning of the step seven times, then step up through the first A added, the next F in the previous round, and the second A added **(Fig. 7, black thread)**.

8. Pick up 1A and 1B. Stitch through the first B in the group of 3B on top of the rose montée. Skip the middle B and stitch through the third. Pick up 1B and 1A and stitch through the next A. Weave through the next F and A **(Fig. 8, black thread)**. Repeat from the beginning of the step seven times **(Fig. 8, red thread)**.

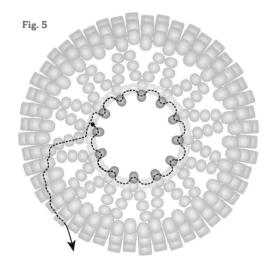

Fig. 5

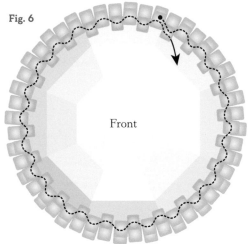

Fig. 6

Front

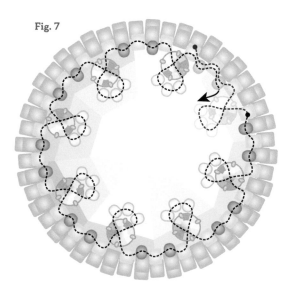

Fig. 7

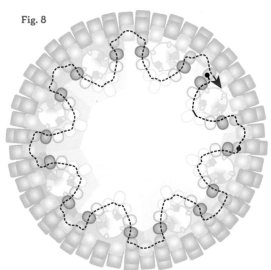

Fig. 8

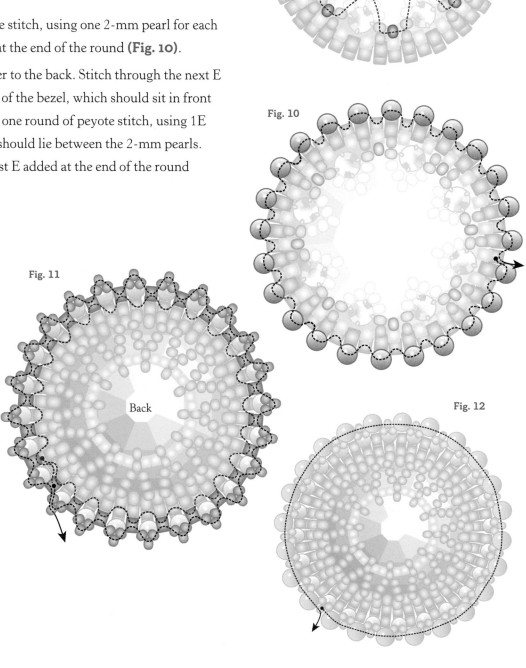

9. Stitch through the next A, the next 4B (skipping the middle B on top of the rose montée again) and the next A **(Fig. 9, blue thread)**. *Pick up 1C. Stitch through the next A, the next 4B (skipping the middle B again), and the next A. Repeat from * seven times **(Fig. 9, red thread)**. Stitch through the next A, F, and 2E so that your thread emerges from the second round of E, counting from the center of the bezel **(Fig. 9, black thread)**.

10. Work a round of peyote stitch, using one 2-mm pearl for each stitch. Do not step up at the end of the round **(Fig. 10)**.

11. Turn the beadwork over to the back. Stitch through the next E toward the back center of the bezel, which should sit in front of a 2-mm pearl. Work one round of peyote stitch, using 1E for each stitch; each E should lie between the 2-mm pearls. Step up through the first E added at the end of the round **(Fig. 11, red thread)**.

12. Pick up 3A. Stitch through the next E. Repeat from the beginning 23 times, then step up through the first 2A added **(Fig. 11, black thread)**.

13. Pick up one 3-mm pearl and stitch through the middle A in the next group of 3A. Repeat 23 times. Do not step up (**Fig. 12**).

Fig. 9

Fig. 10

Fig. 11

Back

Fig. 12

14. Pick up 6A. Stitch through the middle A in the next group of 3A so that the new A wraps around the outside of the 3-mm pearl. Stitch back through the last A added in the group of 6A. *Pick up 5A. Stitch through the middle A in the next group of 3A, then stitch back through the last A added in the group of five. Repeat from * 22 times. To complete the round, pick up 4A and stitch into the very first A added in this round. Stitch through the middle A in the group of 3A in the previous round, then stitch back through the first A added in this round. Step up through the next 2A **(Fig. 13, red thread)**.

15. Pick up 1B. Stitch through the next 2A, skip the sideways A between the 3-mm pearls, and stitch through the next 2A. Repeat from the beginning of the step 23 times, then step up through the first B added **(Fig. 13, black thread)**.

16. Pick up one 4-mm round and stitch through the next B. Repeat 23 times, then step up through the first 4-mm round added **(Fig. 14, blue thread)**. Pull tightly, but be careful—the holes in the crystal rounds can be sharp enough to cut the thread. Repeat the thread path once to reinforce.

17. Pick up 1B and stitch through the next 4-mm round. Repeat 23 times, then step up through the first B added **(Fig. 14, black thread)**. Repeat the thread path once, pulling tightly but carefully. Leave any working thread hanging for assembly. Weave in, secure, and trim your tail thread.

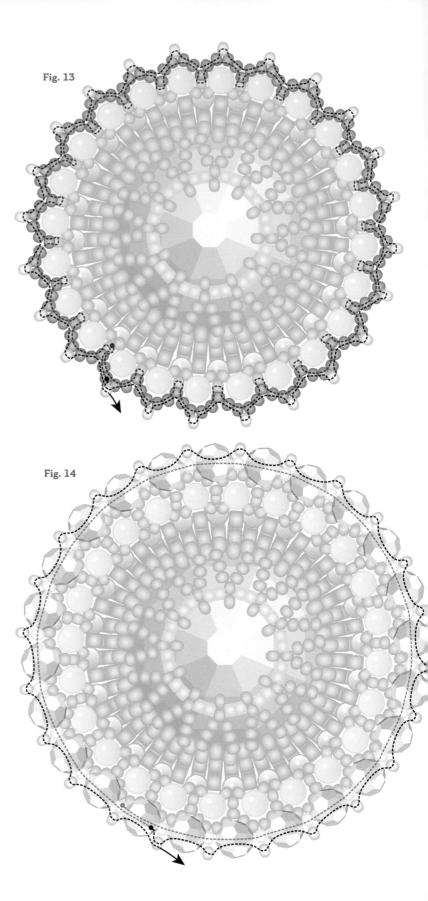

Fig. 13

Fig. 14

Make the Gibbous Moon Components

Fig. 15

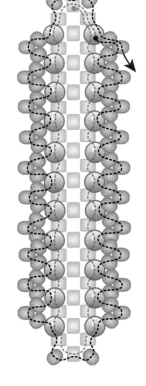

18. Needle up a wingspan of thread. Create a flat strip of 12 RAW units with 4E in each unit, leaving the tail thread just long enough to weave into the beadwork later and trim.

19. Stitch through the next E so your thread is heading toward the start of the strip. Pick up one 2-mm pearl and stitch through the corresponding E in the next unit. Repeat ten times, then stitch through the next 2E. Add eleven 2-mm pearls in the same fashion on the other side of the strip. The pearls on each side should line up. Stitch through the next 2E, then step up through the first 2-mm pearl added **(Fig. 15, blue thread)**.

20. Pick up 3D and stitch through the next 2-mm pearl. Repeat nine times, then stitch through the next E. Pick up 1D and stitch through the next E. Pick up 1D and stitch through the next E and 2-mm pearl. Repeat from the beginning of the step to add ten groups of 3D to the other side of the strip and 2D at the t=other end. Step up through the first 2D added **(Fig. 15, black thread)**. After you complete this step, your strip will start to curve.

21. Pick up one 3-mm pearl and stitch through the middle D in the next group of 3D. Repeat eight times **(Fig. 16)**.

22. You will attach the sides of the RAW strip together to create the outside edge of the component. Pick up 1D. Stitch through the middle D in the group of 3D on the opposite side of the RAW strip. Continue stitching through the next 3-mm pearl and the middle D in the next group of 3D on the side of the RAW strip from which you started. When you reach the other end of the strip, pick up 1D, then stitch through the next D in the first group of 3D added during the previous step, and the next 3-mm pearl **(Fig. 17)**.

Fig. 16

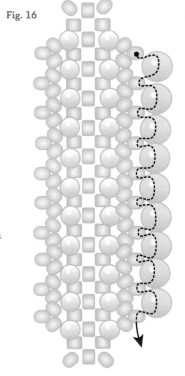

Fig. 17

23. Pick up 1E and stitch through the next 3-mm pearl. Repeat seven times. Stitch through the next 2D so your thread is emerging from the D at the end of the strip **(Fig. 18)**.

24. Pick up 3A and stitch through the D between 2E on the end of the RAW strip. Pick up 3B and stitch through the next D. Pick up 3A and stitch through the D at which you started. *Pick up 4A and stitch through the next E between 3-mm pearls. Repeat from * nine times. Pick up 3A and stitch through the D between the 2E on the opposite end of the RAW strip. Pick up 3B and stitch through the next D. Pick up 3A and stitch through the middle D at the end of the 3-mm pearls **(Fig. 19, black thread)**. Stitch through the next group of 3A and the next D and E **(Fig. 19, pink thread)**.

25. Set one of your 14-mm stones. Place the stone in a brass setting, foil side down. Make sure the stone is sitting evenly against the setting on all sides. Carefully push each of the setting's prongs down against the stone using pliers.

26. Your thread should be emerging from an E in the last RAW unit made of E. Stitch through the next E in the unit, moving your thread towards the back of the bezel, the next 2-mm pearl, and the next E. Place your set stone facedown along the inside edge of the beadwork; the two holes in each side of the setting should align with the sides of the RAW strip. Stitch through the top set of holes in the setting and through the corresponding E in the second to last RAW unit on the other end of the strip. Stitch back through the top set of holes and the E on the first side **(Fig. 20, pink thread)**. Repeat the thread path at least twice to strengthen. Weave through the next 2-mm pearl and the next E. Stitch through the bottom set of holes in the setting and through the corresponding E on the other side. Stitch back through the bottom set of holes and the first E **(Fig. 20, black thread)**. Repeat this thread path at least twice as well.

Fig. 18   Fig. 19

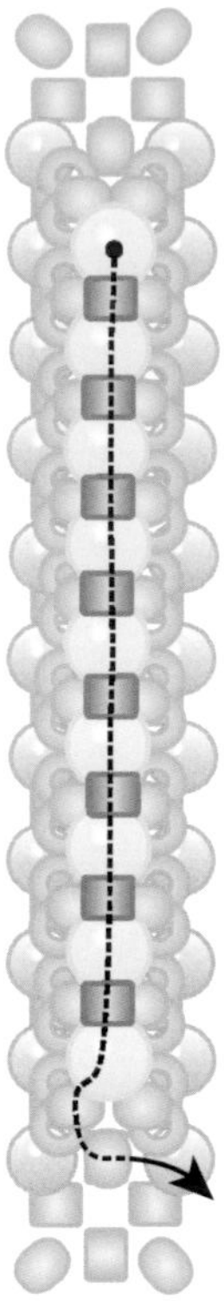

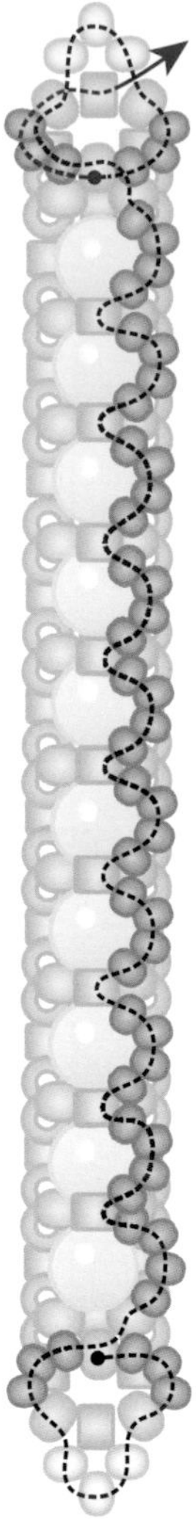

Fig. 20

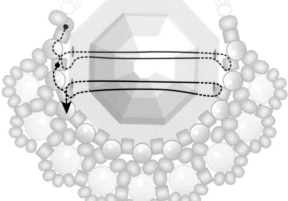

27. Weave through your beadwork so that your thread is emerging from an E in the last RAW unit on either end of the RAW strip on the front side of the bezel. Your thread should be heading toward the other end of the strip. Pick up 1F. Stitch through the next E, then pick up one rose montée and 3B. *Holding the rose montée faceup against the 14-mm stone, stitch through the other hole and the next E. Repeat from * four times to add additional groups of rose montées and 3B. Pick up 1F and stitch through the next E **(Fig. 21, black thread)**. Catch a thread between two beads or tie a half hitch knot by catching the thread between two beads and then stitching underneath the working thread before pulling tightly, then immediately stitch back through the last E and F **(Fig. 21, pink thread)**.

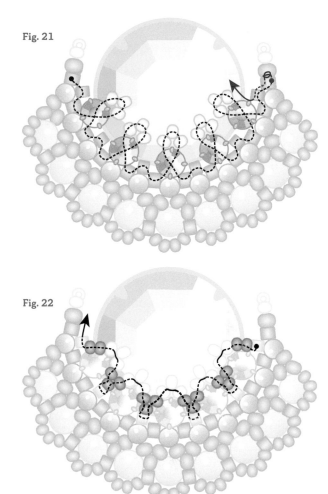

Fig. 21

Fig. 22

28. Pick up 2A. Stitch through the next B on top of the rose montée, skip the following B, and stitch through the third B. Pick up 2A and stitch through the next F. Stitch back through the last A added. *Pick up 1A. Stitch through the next B on top of the rose montée, skip the next B, and stitch through the third B. Pick up 2A. Stitch through the next F, then stitch back through the last A. Repeat from * three times, but on the third repeat, do not stitch back through the last A **(Fig. 22)**. Leave any working thread hanging for assembly later. Weave in, secure, and trim the tail thread.

29. Repeat steps 18–28 to make a second gibbous moon component.

Make the Quarter Moon Components

30. You'll make the Quarter Moon Components using the same method outlined for the Gibbous Moon Components. Needle up a wingspan of thread. Create a flat strip of 10 RAW units with 4E in each unit, leaving just enough tail thread to weave into the beadwork later and trim.

31. Follow steps 21–25 to create the beadwork to surround the stone and setting. Set another 14-mm stone into a brass setting. Working on the back side, stitch through the top set of holes in the setting and through the corresponding E in the second to last RAW unit on the other end of the strip. Stitch back through

the bottom set of holes and the E on the end of the RAW strip at which you started **(Fig. 23)**. Leave any working thread hanging for assembly. Weave in, secure, and trim the tail thread.

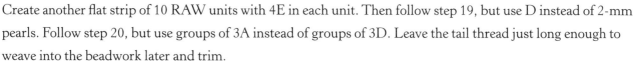

Fig. 23

32. Repeat steps 30 and 31 to make a second quarter moon component.

Make the Crescent Moon Components

33. You'll make the Crescent Moon Components using the same method outlined for the Gibbous Moon Components as well. Needle up a wingspan of thread. Create another flat strip of 10 RAW units with 4E in each unit. Then follow step 19, but use D instead of 2-mm pearls. Follow step 20, but use groups of 3A instead of groups of 3D. Leave the tail thread just long enough to weave into the beadwork later and trim.

34. Pick up one 3-mm pearl and stitch through the middle D in the next group of 3D. Repeat eight times.

35. You will attach the sides of the RAW strip together to create the outside edge of the component. Pick up 1A. Stitch through the middle A in the group of 3A on the opposite side of the RAW strip. Continue stitching through the next 3-mm pearl and the middle A in the next group of 3A, on the side of the RAW strip from which you started. When you reach the other end of the strip, pick up 1A, then stitch through the middle A in the first group of 3A added during the previous step, and the next 3-mm pearl.

36. Pick up 1D and stitch through the next 3-mm pearl. Repeat five times. Stitch through the next 2A, D, and 3E so your thread is headed back toward the last pearl through which you stitched.

37. Turn the beadwork over to the back. Set another 14-mm stone. Holding the stone facedown, stitch through the top set of holes in the setting and through the corresponding E in the last RAW unit on the other end of the strip. Stitch back through the top set of holes and the E on the side in which you started. Repeat the thread path at least twice to strengthen. Weave through the next D and the next E. Stitch through the bottom set of holes in the setting and through the corresponding E on the other end of the strip. Stitch back through the bottom set of holes and the first E **(Fig. 24)**. Repeat this thread path at least twice as well.

Fig. 24

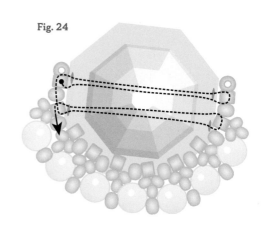

38. Bring your thread out of the last E on one end of the RAW strip. Pick up 7D and stitch through the same E again to form a loop **(Fig. 25)**. Repeat the thread path at least twice to reinforce. Weave in, secure, and trim all threads on the component.

39. Repeat steps 33–38 to make a second crescent moon component, making sure to attach the loop created in step 38 on the side opposite from the first loop.

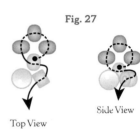

Fig. 25

Make the New Moon Component

40. Needle up a wingspan and a half of thread. Pick up 1D, 1E, and one 2-mm pearl. Stitch through the first D to form a loop, leaving just enough tail thread to weave into the beadwork later **(Fig. 26)**. Stitch around through all three beads once more. This is the base for the first PRAW-3 unit.

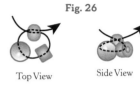

Fig. 26

Top View   Side View

41. For the first side of your PRAW-3 unit, pick up 3D and stitch through the D again and the next E in the base **(Fig. 27)**.

42. For the second side, pick up one 3-mm pearl and 1E. Working toward the base, stitch through the side D in the previous group of 3D and through the E at which you started this step **(Fig. 28, pink thread)**. Stitch through the next 2-mm pearl in the base and the side D in the first group of 3D added **(Fig. 28, black thread)**.

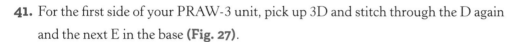

Fig. 27

Top View   Side View

43. For the third side, pick up one 2-mm pearl and stitch back through the 3-mm pearl, working toward the base. Stitch through the next 2-mm pearl in the base and the D at which you started this step **(Fig. 29)**.

Fig. 28   Fig. 29

Side View   Side View

44. Step up through the next D, which is at the top of the unit **(Fig. 30)**. The three beads at the top should be the D, a 2-mm pearl, and an E; they form the base for the next PRAW unit.

45. Repeat steps 41-44 ten times for a total of 11 PRAW units.

Fig. 30   Fig. 31a   Fig. 31b

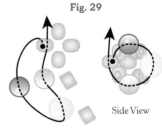

46. The 12th unit will join the first unit to the 11th unit. Pick up 1D and stitch through the D at the base of the first unit. Pick up 1D and stitch through the D and the next E at the top of the 11th unit **(Fig. 31a)**. Pick up one 3-mm pearl and stitch through the E in the base of the first unit. Stitch through the first D added on the previous side, the E in the top of the 11th unit again, and the next 2-mm pearl on the top of the 11th unit **(Fig. 31b)**. Stitch through the second D

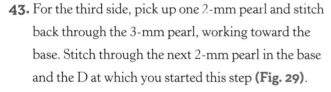

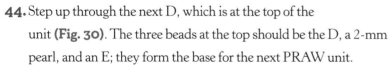

added in this step, the 2-mm pearl in the base of the first unit, and the 3-mm pearl just added, then pass through the 2-mm pearl in the top of the 11th unit again. Stitch through the D added in this step once more **(Fig. 31c)**.

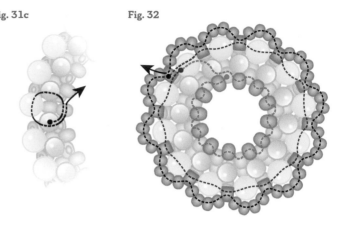

Fig. 31c

Fig. 32

47. On the front of the PRAW ring (the side with the 2-mm pearls showing), work one round of peyote stitch, using 1D for each stitch, along the innermost round of D. Weave through your beadwork to exit through the nearest 3-mm pearl **(Fig. 32, blue thread)**. Work one round of peyote stitch, using 1E for each stitch; step up through the first E added **(Fig. 32, pink thread)**. Work a round of netting, using 4A for each stitch and stitching through each E added in the previous round; do not step up **(Fig. 32, black thread)**.

48. Pick up 15A and the navette pendant. The hole in the navette pendant will be larger than the other beads on your thread; move the pendant on your thread until it rests on the center 3A of the group of 15A. Stitch back through the E from which your thread is emerging **(Fig. 33, pink thread)**. Stitch through the next 3-mm pearl and 2-mm pearl, working toward the inside of the ring. Moving toward the E where you started, stitch through the next 5D, then the next 2-mm pearl toward the outside of the ring, and the next 3-mm pearl back toward the pendant. Stitch through the next E; it should be the one nearest to the E where you began **(Fig. 33, black thread)**.

Fig. 33

Fig. 34

49. Pick up 6A. Stitch through the 3A in the middle of the previous group of 15A (they should be the ones in the navette pendant's hole). Pick up 6A and stitch back through the E from where your thread first emerged **(Fig. 34)**. Repeat the thread path once more to reinforce. Weave in, secure, and trim all hanging threads.

Assembly

Fig. 35

50. Needle up the hanging thread on the Full Moon Component. It should be emerging from a B just before one of the 4-mm rounds aligned with a rose montée. If not, weave to the nearest B. Pick up 21D and pass your needle through the center of the New Moon Component. Then stitch through the same B on the Full Moon Component again **(Fig. 35, black thread)**, the next 4-mm round, and the next B **(Fig. 35, pink thread)**.

51. Repeat the previous step to add a second loop of D through the New Moon Component. Repeat all thread paths as many times as possible to reinforce.

52. Weave your working thread through the 4-mm rounds and the B in the Full Moon Component until you reach the B between the third and fourth 4-mm round from the top center of the component. Orient one Gibbous Moon Component so it is facing up with the stone above the beadwork. Pick up 1A. Working in the direction away from the end of the RAW strip, stitch through the third and fourth A in the group of 4A on the end of the Gibbous Moon Component. Stitch through the next E and the next 2A. Pick up 1A. Stitch through the next B on the Full Moon Component after the fourth 4-mm round from the center **(Fig. 36, black thread)**. Stitch back through the new A, 2A, E, and 2A on the Gibbous Moon Component, and the other new A. Stitch through the B on the Full Moon Component between the third and fourth 4-mm rounds from top center **(Fig. 36, pink thread)**. Repeat the thread path at least twice for security. Weave to the opposite side of the Full Moon Component and attach the other Gibbous Moon Component in the same manner. Weave in, secure, and trim your thread.

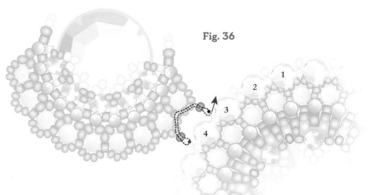

Fig. 36

53. To connect a Gibbous Moon Component to a Quarter Moon Component, needle up the working thread on the Gibbous Moon Component. Heading toward the end of the RAW strip, weave to the third A in the last group of 4A opposite the 4A that serve as the attachment point between the Gibbous Moon Component and the Full Moon Component. Place the Quarter Moon Component next to the Gibbous Moon Component as shown in **Figure 37**. Pick up 1A and stitch through the middle 2A in the group of 4A at the end of the Quarter Moon Component. Pick up 1A and stitch through the middle 2A in the group of 4A on the end of the Gibbous Moon Component **(Fig. 37)**. Repeat the thread path at least twice to reinforce. Weave in, secure, and trim your thread. Repeat from the beginning of this step to secure the remaining Quarter Moon Component on the opposite side of the necklace.

Fig. 37

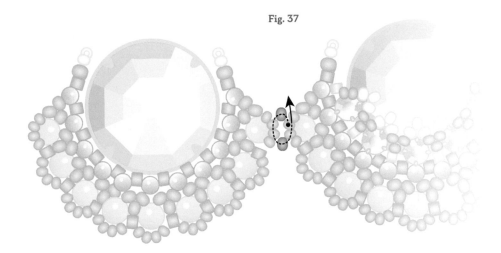

54. To connect a Crescent Moon Component to a Quarter Moon Component, needle up the working thread on the Quarter Moon Component. Place the Crescent Moon Component next to the Gibbous Moon Component with the stone on top of the beadwork and facing up. Weave to the middle 2A in the last group of 4A headed toward the end of the RAW strip, opposite the 4A that serve as an attachment point between the Gibbous Moon Component and Quarter Moon Component. Pick up 1A and stitch through the last 3-mm pearl away from the end of the RAW strip. Pick up 2A and stitch through the middle 2A in the group of 4A at the end of the Quarter Moon Component. Repeat the thread path at least twice to reinforce. Weave in, secure, and trim your thread. Repeat from the beginning of this step to secure the remaining Crescent Moon Component on the opposite side of the necklace.

55. Cut the chain in two equal lengths with wire cutters. Open a jump ring by rotating two pairs of pliers in opposite directions. Load the end link of one chain half onto the jump ring, then close the ring around the loop of D on one end of the necklace assembly. Repeat with the other jump ring and chain half on the other end of the necklace. To add the closure, open the bottom loop of the clasp hook with two pairs of pliers. Load the end link of one chain half onto it, then close the jump ring.

Variations: Use the following beads to create these color variations.

Bronze Necklace

A: Metallic bronze size 15° seed beads

B: 24-karat gold-plated size 15° seed beads

C: Gold-lined frosted crystal size 15° seed beads

D: Metallic bronze size 11° seed beads

E: Metallic golden olive iris size 10° cylinder beads

F: Metallic golden olive iris size 11° cylinder beads

2-mm glass pearl: Purple

3-mm crystal pearl: Iridescent green

4-mm crystal rounds: Amethyst 2XAB

Rose montée: Scarabaceous green

23-mm Solaris stone: Iridescent green

14-mm Solaris stone: Iridescent green

30-mm pendant: Golden shadow

Settings: Natural brass

Silver Necklace

A: Palladium-plated size 15° seed beads

B: Bright sterling-plated size 15° seed beads

C: Metallic gunmetal size 15° seed beads

D: Matte bright sterling-plated size 11° cylinder beads

E: Matte nickel-plated size 10° cylinder beads

F: Nickel-plated size 11° cylinder beads

2-mm glass pearl: Gray

3-mm crystal pearl: Iridescent dark blue

4-mm crystal rounds: White opal

Rose montée: Air blue opal/silver

23-mm Solaris stone: Crystal

14-mm Solaris stone: Mystique

30-mm pendant: Blue shade

Settings: Rhodium-plated

Gallery

« *Aurelio Castaño and Edwin Batres*

KORALES NECKLACE, 2018

48.3 x 11.4 x 1.3 cm

Seed beads, crystal pearls, natural coral, sterling silver chain, sterling silver end caps, sterling silver hook clasp; peyote stitch, netting, right-angle weave, cubic right-angle weave

Photo by Edwin Batres

Jayashree Paramesh »

QUEEN OF THE LAKES NECKLACE, 2017

48.3 x 6.4 cm

Seed beads, cylinder beads, crystal stone, crystal beads and pearls, glass bead; prismatic right-angle weave, netting, peyote stitch

Photo by Jayashree Paramesh

« *Heather Kingsley-Heath*

THE GIRL WITH A SCORPION CORSAGE (A COSTUME DRAMA), 2012

20.3 x 22.9 x 10.2 cm

Seed beads, crystal beads, shaped glass beads, wire and metal findings, textile; Albion stitch, herringbone stitch, netting

Photo by Heather Kingsley-Heath

« *Nancy Cain*

DRAGONFLY ORNAMENT, 2002

12.7 cm x 14 cm x 12.7 cm

Seed beads, crystal beads; tubular peyote
stitch, peyote stitch

Photo by Dave Wolverton

⩔ *Laura McCabe*

EYEBALL FLOWER CREATURE SCULPTURE, 2017

8.9 x 8.9 x 8.9 cm

Seed beads, crystal beads, glass doll eyes, cut fossil
coral, freshwater pearls; tubular peyote stitch,
peyote stitch

Photo by Melinda Holden

« *Diane Hyde*

CLOUD EMPRESS NECKLACE, 2016

16.5 x 13.3 cm

Seed beads, crystal beads, face cabochon,
freshwater pearls, wire neckband, Ultrasuede®,
beading foundation; peyote stitch, bead
embroidery, fringing

Photo by Diane Hyde

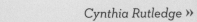

« *Cindy Holsclaw*

FRAMED ART BLOSSOMS NECKLACE, 2017

43.2 x 5.1 cm

Seed beads, shaped glass beads; peyote stitch, prismatic right-angle weave

Photo by Cindy Holsclaw

Cynthia Rutledge »

BUTTERFLY KISSES BRACELET, 2018

6.4 x 6.4 x 3.8 cm

Seed beads, cylinder beads, crystal pearls; tubular peyote stitch, flat peyote stitch, peyote stitch variations

Photo by Mark Rutledge

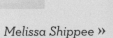

Betty Stephan ⌃

CHANGES NECKLACE, 2014

22.9 x 20.3 x 1.3 cm

Cabochons by Laurie Leonard, glass beads, seed beads, leather backing; tubular peyote stitch, fringing

Photo by Betty Stephan

Melissa Shippee »

SWEET SUMMER CHILD HEADDRESS, 2016

20.3 x 17.8 cm

Seed beads, crystal stones, crystal beads, crystal pearls, beading foundation, ribbon; bead embroidery, prismatic right-angle weave, peyote stitch

Photo by Melissa Shippee

Acknowledgments

Writing this book has been no small undertaking, and it wouldn't have been possible without the constant support of my husband, Matthew Shippee, who has always been willing to wrangle children, run errands, stay up late, and go the extra mile to support my creative endeavors.

It takes a team of people to bring a technical book like this to fruition, and I have to thank my editor at Sterling Publishing, Elysia Liang, for all her hard work, patience, and countless hours she poured into this endeavor. I also must thank my technical editor, Cathy Jakicic, for her dedication through multiple rounds of edits, and for being so understanding of my crazy and often last-minute schedule. Thank you also to the other members of the team at Sterling for their hard work and expertise: Scott Amerman, Shannon Plunkett, Lorie Pagnozzi, Chris Bain, David Ter-Avanesyan, and Fred Pagan.

For enriching my book with their creativity and unique ideas, thank you to my friends and colleagues who have submitted their work to the Gallery section for allowing me to showcase their unique voices, and for being nothing but supportive and encouraging with my own work.

About the Author

Melissa Shippee has been fascinated with nature for her entire life, spending countless hours outside observing the natural world around her. Encouraged by her parents, she developed an early interest in drawing and painting that won her numerous accolades at school. In college, she first studied biology and physics, then added a fine arts degree in painting to explore her artistic interests further. Melissa later discovered beadweaving and was captivated by creating tiny works of art that channel her passion for engineering beautiful objects and explaining how they are made.

Melissa's beading obsession quickly became a career. Since 2007, she has traveled the world to teach beading workshops, published how-to articles in beading magazines such as *Perlen Poesie, Bead Star, Beadwork,* and *Bead & Button,* and was *Beadwork* magazine's Designer of the Year in 2017. She has won awards in multiple design contests and drawn diagrams for top designers' tutorials and books. To view more of Melissa's work, visit her website at mgsdesigns.net.

Index

Note: Page numbers in *italics* indicate projects.